Write
your own
Magic

Make Your Hopes and Dreams Come True

We all have hopes and dreams, and this book will show you how to use the power of words to turn your desires into reality. There is no limit to what you can ask for, as long as your requests hurt no one. For instance, you might want:

- vibrant health
- a fulfilling relationship
- greater happiness
- more money
- a better job
- stronger faith
- increased creativity and intuition

All of this, and much more, can be brought into your life when you follow the step-by-step instructions in this magical guidebook. *Write Your Own Magic* will show you how to create original white magic spells that make your hopes and dreams come true.

About the Author

Richard Webster was born in New Zealand in 1946, and he resides there still. He travels widely every year, lecturing and conducting workshops on psychic subjects around the world. He has written many books, mainly on psychic subjects, and also writes monthly magazine columns. Richard is married with three children. His family is very supportive of his occupation, but his oldest son, after watching his father's career, has decided to become an accountant.

Many of Llewellyn's authors have websites with additional information and resources. For more information, please visit our website at:

http://www.llewellyn.com

Write your own Magic

The Hidden Power in Your Words

Richard Webster

2001
Llewellyn Publications
St. Paul, Minnesota 55164-0383, U.S.A.

First Edition
First Printing, 2001

Book design and editing by Joanna Willis
Cover design by Kevin R. Brown
Cover photo © Doug Deutscher

Library of Congress Cataloging-in-Publication Data
Webster, Richard
  Write your own magic: the hidden power in your words /
Richard Webster
     p. cm.
  Includes bibliographical references and index.
  ISBN 0-7387-0001-0
     1. Magic. 2. Success—Miscellanea. I. Title.

BF1611 .W434 2001
131—dc21
                                                              2001023440

Llewellyn Publications
A Division of Llewellyn Worldwide, Ltd.
P.O. Box 64383, Dept. 0-7387-0001-0
St. Paul, MN 55164-0383, U.S.A.
www.llewellyn.com

 Printed in the United States of America on recycled paper

Other Books by Richard Webster

Astral Travel for Beginners

Aura Reading for Beginners

The Complete Book of Palmistry

Dowsing for Beginners

Feng Shui for Apartment Living

Feng Shui for Beginners

Feng Shui for Love & Romance

Feng Shui for Success & Happiness

Feng Shui for the Workplace

Feng Shui in the Garden

Numerology Magic

Omens, Oghams & Oracles

101 Feng Shui Tips for the Home

Palm Reading for Beginners

Seven Secrets to Success

Soul Mates

Spirit Guides & Angel Guardians

Success Secrets

Forthcoming

Practical Guide to Past-Life Memories

For Ron Martin;
author, raconteur, gifted palmist, and good friend.

Contents

Contents

Contents

Introduction

Words were originally magic and to this day words have retained much of their ancient magical power.

SIGMUND FREUD (1856–1939)

When you were a child, I am sure you were familiar with the saying "Sticks and stones may break my bones, but names will never hurt me." This rhyme may have been a useful retaliation when people called you names, but unfortunately the message is quite untrue. Names can hurt you. The power of the spoken word is immense.

The power of words is incredible. The fact that we can communicate with each other in words is one of the main reasons why humanity has progressed so much further than any other living beings on this planet. Writing that reproduced language began in Mesopotamia and Egypt and dates back only five thousand years. However, writing in the broadest sense of the word goes back tens of thousands of years.[1]

Whenever writing appeared it was accompanied by a huge blossoming of commerce, industry, arts, and government that totally transformed everyone's way of life. Consequently, writing was one of the most important factors in the creation of the great civilizations.

Writing was considered so important that its origins were almost always ascribed to a god by ancient cultures. The Mesopotamians had the goddess Nisaba, the Babylonians Nabu, the Egyptians Thoth, and so on. In the East, the Chinese credit Wu of Hsia with the invention of writing.[2] In Islam, God is believed to have created writing. Hindus credit Brahma with writing. In the Norse legends, Odin created the runes. In the druidic tradition, Ogma invented the ogham alphabet.[3]

The Greeks were almost alone in not ascribing a divine origin to writing. This was because educated Greeks were able to read and write, and had no need to give writing the mystical element that was common in places where few people were able to read or write.

Writing has changed enormously over time. It is only in the last three hundred years that we have been writing in the form we use today. You would have no difficulty reading something that was hand-written by Charles Dickens (nineteenth century), Joseph Addison (eighteenth century) or John Milton (seventeenth century). However, you would find it almost impossible to read William Shakespeare's handwriting (sixteenth century) because you would be unable to decipher any of the individual letters.[4]

The power of the written word is incredible. Imagine how magical words on paper must seem to someone who is illiterate. Although they look like meaningless squiggles, everyone who reads them out loud would say exactly the same thing. That is magic!

Many people today consider magic to be a primitive form of science, but it cannot be dismissed that easily. In fact, the boundaries between science and magic are vague and undefined. When we turn on a light, we know that electricity is involved, but we need not know anything about power or electricity for it to happen. We have faith that when we press the switch, the light will come on. Few people know anything about the latest advances in physics or medicine, but we have faith that these researches will help us.

We are aware that many things that we implicitly believed in just fifty years ago have been discredited. Fifty years from now, some of the things we believe in today will seem just as ludicrous. Belief is a powerful part of magic, but it also plays an equally important role in science.

According to *The Unabridged Random House Dictionary of the English Language,* magic is the art of achieving a desired result by the use of certain mysterious techniques, such as incantations or ceremonies. Magic also uses enchantments, power, influence, and spells to help achieve a desired goal. We will be using all of these techniques to help you create magic in your own life.

The concept of writing your own magic is extremely old. Thousands of years ago, the ancient Egyptians used to write letters to the dead, asking them to influence events in the world of the living. Usually these letters were written on a bowl in which bread or grain would be placed, but papyrus and cloth were also used. The Egyptians believed that the spirits of the dead were simply travelling and could intercede and help when asked to do so. Consequently, family members who were squabbling, for example, could write to their deceased mother and ask her to resolve the situation. One famous existing example is the letter that a widower wrote to his dead wife. He had mourned her death for three years and still felt no lessening of anguish. He felt that she had bewitched him from beyond the grave, and wrote to her asking to be set free.[5] The ancient Egyptians used the power of the written word to create changes, or magic, in their lives.

Traditionally, magicians taught their secrets by word of mouth, from master to student. Anything that was written down was kept well hidden and out of the hands of the uninitiated. The invention of the printing press changed all that. In the Middle Ages a series of grimoires were produced containing magical secrets from the Persian, Hebrew, Christian, and magical traditions. Probably the most famous of these grimoires is the *Key of Solomon*, which gives full details of the seventy-two spirits that were invoked by King Solomon.

Cryptography, or secret writing, is not a science that has been practiced only by spies. In fact, ancient magicians regularly used it to keep their mysteries a secret. The Celts had their oghams, which were intended to keep valuable information away from "the vulgar and poor of the nations."[6] The Egyptians had their hieroglyphs, which were used only for sacred writing,[7] and the Greeks had their scytalus, which was used when information had to be kept secret.[8]

Faith in the power and efficacy of written and spoken words has been recorded in the history of most cultures. The use of prayer wheels in Tibet is possibly the most striking example of this.[9] A prayer wheel is a hollow, metal cylinder mounted on a rod. This cylinder is usually beautifully engraved. A prayer or mantra is written on a roll of paper, fabric, or parchment that is consecrated by a lama before being inserted into the prayer wheel. The handle of the prayer wheel is rotated to set the prayer wheel into motion. Each revolution of the wheel is believed to equal saying the mantra out loud once. However, as the prayer wheel is not believed to be as powerful as the spoken voice, the wheel needs to be revolved more frequently to recapture this lost power. The person turning the wheel needs to concentrate on the task to ensure that the correct beneficial results are attained. Prayer flags serve the same purpose when they are blowing in the wind.

The Tibetan people still write their own magic in a variety of different ways. In 1981, the 16th Karmapa Lama placed a coded message in a letter that he concealed inside an amulet. He gave this amulet to his teacher, Tai Situpa Rinpoche, for safekeeping. The amulet had to be carefully looked after as the coded message gave details about his birthplace in his next reincarnation.[10]

In this book we are going to use words to enable you to manifest in your life whatever you desire. We all have dreams, hopes, and wishes. Sadly, though, for the most part these remain as dreams, hopes, and wishes. However with the information in this book, you can use the magical power of words to allow you to achieve your desires and lead a life of happiness, success, and fulfillment.

Happiness is the state of being contented with one's lot. It is hard to define it further than this since something that makes you happy may not have the same effect on someone else. However, two things are extremely important in leading a full, happy, and worthwhile life: One, you must be true to yourself. You will never find true happiness if you spend your life trying to live up to the expectations of others and ignoring what your own heart is telling you. The second is that you must strive toward making your dreams a reality.

Bob, an acquaintance of mine, spent thirty years as an insurance salesman. He did reasonably well at it, but never felt fulfilled or happy. As a child he had been interested in puppetry and had a little marionette theater. This passion of his gradually faded during his teenage years, but it returned when his own children were small. He began making puppets again and performed little shows for his children and their friends. One day, I happened to visit while he was performing. I was impressed by the quality of the entire show. The small theater and puppets were beautiful, and Bob had written a charming story for the figures to act out. The children were mesmerized by the performance, and their parents were captivated as well. I was amazed at the expression on Bob's face. He appeared completely transformed, and he had a radiant air about him. Afterwards, I suggested that he market his act and do it professionally.

Bob shook his head. "That was my dream as a child," he told me. "But I could never do it now."

"Why not?" I asked.

Bob shrugged. "I'm too old. I wouldn't know how to begin. I couldn't make enough money to feed my family with it."

I listened as he went through a list of reasons why he could never do it. When he finished, I commented on how his whole appearance and personality had changed while he was performing.

"You've found your passion," I said. "You have to do something with it."

I told him some of the ideas that are in this book, and he listened with interest. By the time I left, Bob had agreed to have some business cards printed, but I never for a moment thought that he would give up his lucrative career in insurance to become a children's entertainer. Much to my surprise, Bob began marketing his act. The first I knew of this was when a local shopping mall advertised that he would be entertaining the children there for one week during the summer vacation. Naturally, I went to see his show.

It had developed greatly, and Bob had allowed his personality to blossom. His show attracted hundreds of people, most of whom stayed until the end even though they had come to the mall for other purposes. Afterwards, Bob told me that he had given up insurance and was doing puppetry full time. His enthusiasm was infectious.

"I have to thank you," he said, "for making me see that I could live my dream. I wish I'd done it twenty years ago."

We all wish that we could have done things years before, but I believe that everything happens when the time is right. Bob may not have succeeded as a puppeteer if he had tried to do it earlier on in his life. During the previous twenty years he had learned a great deal about life and business, and was able to use those skills in his new venture. Also, by finally following his dream in middle life, he appreciated his success much more than he would have if it had happened at the age of twenty.

Bob used many of the techniques in this book. He finally gave up fulfilling other people's expectations and began to listen to what his heart told him. He also followed the four steps explained in this book to create a plan that made his dreams become a reality.

Over the years, I have explained these ideas to people of all ages. I have given talks on this subject in both high schools and retirement homes. I know they will work for you, no matter how young or old you may be. It saddens me to meet so many people who are not following their true path. It is never too late to find your passion and make it happen. Follow the ideas in this book, write your own magic, and fulfill your dreams.

In this book I describe methods of writing your own magic that I have used myself. There are other methods of writing your own magic that I have not experimented with. For instance, a popular method in Thailand is to tattoo a message on your body.

Many stories have been told about interesting messages that have been tattooed on intimate parts of people's bodies.[11] From what I have heard these methods work, but I have had no personal experience with them, so have not included them.

Words Are Magic

Chapter 1

In the beginning was the Word, and the Word was with God, and the Word was God. The same was in the beginning with God.

THE GOSPEL ACCORDING TO JOHN, 1:1–2

WORDS HOLD ENORMOUS POWER. Good speakers can have us roaring with laughter at one moment, and then seconds later bring tears to our eyes. How do they do this? Naturally, the speakers' actions and facial expressions are involved, but basically they are using words.

Think of the power of the simple words *I love you.* There is a wealth of meaning here that runs well beyond what the words themselves say. The word *home* means so much more than *house,* even though they may both be describing the same thing.

Some words have more power than others. Emotional words such as *love, hate, betrayal, revenge,* and *gluttony* have much more intensity to them than emotionless words such as *cloud, ladder,* and *brick.*

Individual words can mean many different things to different people. The word *car,* for instance, may represent freedom, prestige, and status to a teenager, while for someone else it may simply be a method of getting from one place to another.

However it is not only the individual words that contain power. Even the individual letters that make up the words contain magic. Numerology demonstrates this. Numerology is the ancient art of studying numbers and their meanings. It is usually used to analyze people's names and dates of birth, and is a highly accurate method of character analysis. But it need not be restricted to these purposes, as any word can be interpreted numerologically.

We start by turning the individual letters of the word into numbers using the following chart:

1	2	3	4	5	6	7	8	9
A	B	C	D	E	F	G	H	I
J	K	L	M	N	O	P	Q	R
S	T	U	V	W	X	Y	Z	

We place the vowels above the word, and the consonants below. (The vowels and consonants are separated because it makes it easier to interpret the word later.) Consequently, the word *rabbit*, for example, would look like this:

```
  1   9
RABBIT
9 22 2
```

We then add up the numbers and reduce them to a single digit:

```
  1   9  = 10, and 1 + 0 = 1
RABBIT
9 22 2 = 15, and 1 + 5 = 6
```

In numerology the vowels are called the *Soul Urge*, or *Heart's Desire*. They represent the inner motivation of the word.

The other important aspect of the word is the *Expression* number. This is made up of both the consonants and vowels. It represents the natural potential of the word.

If you look at the word *rabbit* again, you will see that it has a Soul Urge number of 1, and an Expression number of 7 (1 from the vowels + 6 from the consonants).

Unfortunately, there is an exception to the rule. *Y* can be either a consonant or a vowel. If it acts as a vowel or is not pronounced, it is classed as a vowel. If it is pronounced, it is considered a consonant. Consequently, the *y* in *type* and *hay* would be considered a vowel, but in *yacht* and *yellow* it would be classed as a consonant. The word *yesterday* contains two *y*s. One is a consonant, but the other is a vowel.

11 and 22 are considered Master numbers in numerology, and are not reduced down to 2 or 4. Here is an example:

```
   6   5 = 11
HOME
   8   4   = 12, and 1 + 2 = 3
```

Home has a Soul Urge of 11 and an Expression of 5 (11 + 3 = 14, and 1 + 4 = 5).

Meanings of the Numbers

Each number has a meaning.

    1 — Independence and attainment.
    2 — Tact, diplomacy, and intuition.
    3 — Creative self-expression. Experiencing the
        joys of life.
    4 — Limitations and restrictions. System and
        order.
    5 — Freedom, variety.
    6 — Service to others, responsibility.
    7 — Introspection, analysis, spirituality.
    8 — Material freedom. Power.
    9 — Humanitarianism. Concern for others.
   11 — Illumination and inspiration.
   22 — Master builder. Unlimited potential.

If we look at the word *home* again, we see that home is a special place (11 is a Master number) where we can express ourselves freely (5 Expression), and enjoy freedom and variety.

Likewise, *rabbit* is timid (7 Expression) and independent (1 Soul Urge).

Let's look at some more important words.

```
6   3 = 9
LOVE
3   4  = 7
```

Love has an Expression of 7 (9 + 7 = 16, and 1 + 6 = 7), indicating that it is spiritual in nature. It also has a 9 Soul Urge showing it has concern for others.

```
5   = 5
SEX
1 6 = 7
```

Sex has an Expression of 3 which shows that it is creative, joyful, and fun. The Soul Urge of 5 demonstrates freedom and variety. This is why the incredible power of sex has to be channeled carefully.

```
1  5 = 6
HATE
8  2  = 10 = 1
```

This word shows that every number has both a positive and negative interpretation. *Hate* has a 7 Expression which indicates that it is inward looking. This is why people who harbor feelings of hate invariably hurt themselves more than the person they are directing this energy against. It also has a 6 Soul Urge which represents a negative aspect to responsibility and service to others.

Here is an interesting one:

```
  6    = 6
GOD
7   4 = 11
```

God is both powerful and responsible.

```
  6  57 = 18 = 9
MONEY
4   5     = 9
```

```
  1  9   = 10 = 1
MAGIC
4  7 3 = 14 = 5
```

Magic has an Expression number of 6 which shows its responsibility and service to others. It also has a Soul Urge of 1 which indicates that it is independent and self-reliant.

Interestingly enough, *money*'s Expression and Soul Urge numbers are both 9, meaning that in a perfect world it would be used for humanitarian reasons to help others.

The hidden meaning behind any word can be determined in this way. It illustrates the magic that can be found in every word.

Sacred Names

The Chinese have always known the sacred power that the characters of a name possess. In the second millennium B.C.E., priests were the only people who were able to express themselves in writing. They wrote characters on bone and shells which were then heated. The cracks that appeared were interpreted as advice on matters that concerned them, such as when to plant crops and the likelihood of success in battle. Some of these bones and shells still exist today.

The ancient priests constructed the characters with enormous care as they believed that they could express the very essence of the universe with their brushwork. Consequently, these characters express the ideas contained inside them, as well as being a part of what they express. This means that the character for *beautiful,* for example, is also beautiful in itself. The character for *sacred* is sacred, and the character for *prosperity* is prosperous. Some words do not translate exactly. The word *heart,* for instance, actually means the heart and mind in Chinese, because it is the heart that rules human thought and the consequent action.

This is why it is not uncommon in China, particularly on the five sacred mountains, to find a character carved into a rockface.[1] Sometimes a complete poem may be carved into the rock, but more commonly it will be a single word. The people who have painstakingly carved a Chinese character into the rock have written their own magic in the process.

Hidden Names

The ancient Egyptians believed that knowing a name gave a person power. Consequently, hidden names were frequently used to conceal a person's real name from the uninitiated. Even the individual letters of the name are important as they contain vital energy that the person can use.

This tradition is still practiced in modern Egyptian villages where it is considered rude to address a married woman by her real name. Instead, she is known as the mother of her eldest child. This dates back to ancient times, but is still relevant today. In the villages there are "black magicians" who will accept money to write a spell intended to hurt someone. However, this spell will not be effective unless the victim's true name, as well as the victim's mother's name, is known to the magician.[2]

The name was considered so powerful by the ancient Egyptians that the names of enemies were deliberately removed from their tombs and other monuments. Even the names of criminals were changed to unpleasant ones as an additional punishment. The ultimate punishment was to remove someone's name and not replace it, thus condemning them to a second death after physical death.[3] Destroying a person's identity in these ways effectively destroyed the person's life and even created grave dangers in the afterlife.

Followers of the goddess Isis often use a magical name when performing their rites. They can also change their name as they progress if they desire.[4]

There are many legends told about Isis, and one of them explains how she used magic to learn the secret name of Re, the god of light. According to the legend, when Re became old, he dribbled on the ground. Isis obtained this earth and molded it into a serpent. She placed the serpent on the ground beside a path that Re regularly used. When Re walked past, the serpent bit him. Re suffered excruciating pain and could not believe that it had happened. He summoned the children of the gods and asked everyone whose words would reach heaven to come to his aid.

Various people tried to help him, but no one was able to do much until Isis arrived. Isis asked Re for his secret name so that she could create a spell that would keep him alive. He gave her a false name, but the poison remained in his body and his condition worsened. Finally he whispered his secret name to Isis and she effected a cure. To this day, only followers of Isis know Re's secret name.

Today, American Indian Navahos still believe that a person's name should be kept secret. Consequently, it is not used, or even known, by others. If someone's true name were known, sorcery could be used against that person.[5]

All of this shows the magical power that is imprinted in your name. When you write your own magic, you must always sign your name at the end of your request, just as you sign your name when you write a letter to someone. When you write your own magic you are effectively writing a letter to the universe, and consequently, it is of vital importance that you sign it. This adds energy and power to whatever it is you are requesting.

Graphology

Graphology uses the magic of words and takes it still further. Every time you write something down, part of your personality is revealed. Your handwriting reveals your mood, health, vitality, enthusiasm, and much more. People who do not want to attract attention to themselves have small handwriting. People who want attention have large handwriting. People who write slowly and carefully will think in the same sort of way. Quick, spontaneous thinkers will write quickly, as that is natural to them.

The upward strokes of your handwriting reveal your intellect and degree of ambition. The middle zone of your handwriting represents your everyday life. The downward strokes reveal your instinctual drives and sexuality.

The slant of your handwriting reveals how introverted or extroverted you are. If the writing slopes backwards, you are introverted (assuming you are right-handed). The more your writing slopes forward, the more extroverted you are. Interestingly, the same thing applies if you are left-handed. Left-handed writers tend to naturally slope to the left as they push the pen, rather than pull it the way right-handed people do. Despite this, left-handed people curl their wrists and hands around in a way that allows them to write with a slant to the right. This means that left-handed people also indicate their degree of introversion and extroversion in their handwriting.

The degree of pressure that is used reveals the amount of energy available to the writer. A naturally aggressive person will use enormous pressure when writing, while someone who is timid and shy will use light pressure.

Your normal handwriting reveals your personality, but your signature shows what you want the world to see about you. There is a wonderful scene in the film *Shakespeare in Love* where the young William Shakespeare practices different versions of his signature. Most people do this as they are growing up. The size of your signature, compared to the rest of your text, reveals your degree of self-importance. This can, and usually does, vary at different times in your life.

Napoleon Bonaparte's signature is an excellent example of this. As a young man, it was normal in size. Just before he became emperor, it was enormous. Sadly, when he was exiled on Elba his signature was small and ran downward, which is a sign of depression.

Even if you have never studied graphology, you will instinctively recognize all of these things when you look at a piece of writing. We absorb much more information than we realize. A friend of mine has bipolar disorder. When he writes me a letter, a quick glance at his writing on the envelope tells me instantly of his mood. Naturally, I know my friend well. Even with no knowledge of graphology or of a person, you can learn a great deal by examining letters written to you by total strangers.

Because your handwriting reveals so much of your personality, it is important that you use your normal handwriting when writing down your desires. This puts your own personality into the equation, and adds even more power to your request.

Secret Writing

Codes and ciphers have been used for thousands of years to keep information secret. Alchemists were particularly concerned that their secrets might be discovered by people who would not use them responsibly. Of course, they were also considered heretics and had to take great care that their secrets were protected. Consequently, they used a system of complicated codes, along with special locks and secret hiding places to keep their knowledge secret.

The eighth-century Arab alchemist Abu Musa Jabir, also known as Geber, gave his name to the word *gibberish*. Geber was a skilled musician, artist, and mathematician who invented a secret notation system that ultimately gave birth to our modern system of chemical equations.[6] He was unquestionably writing his own magic.

Throughout history, most people have thought that alchemists were solely interested in turning base metal into gold. They must have gotten tired of constantly saying, *"Aurum nostrum non est aurum vulgum"* ("Our gold is not the common gold"). "Our gold" meant the potential, or gold, that lies inside us, rather than the gold traded by goldsmiths. In fact, an alchemist's main goal was to seek a unity between the mind and the body, and to achieve physical and spiritual immortality. It is highly likely that the concept of turning base metal into gold depicted what the alchemists were trying to do with themselves. Ultimately, they wanted to transform themselves into highly evolved, spiritual beings.

The alchemists created a huge library of written and pictorial matter that showed how they wrote their own magic. Their pictures were invariably imaginative and dreamlike. One of their favorite symbols was the *quadratura circuli* ("squaring of the circle").[7] As we will see in chapter 10, this is a good example of a mandala, one of the devices we will be using in writing our own magic.

Eliminating Fear, Doubt, and Worry

Writing is a highly effective way of eliminating problems from our lives. If you have a fear, worry, phobia, or feelings of self-doubt, sit down quietly somewhere and write a letter to yourself. Tell yourself whatever it is that concerns you. You can write down whatever you wish, as no one will see what you have written unless you choose to show it to them. You will be amazed at what you write. All sorts of things that you have not thought about before will come to the surface. This is because you eliminate the normal barrier between your conscious and subconscious minds when writing down your thoughts and feelings freely.

Writing this letter creates order where there was chaos before. You may have had all sorts of vague, unsettling doubts and fears that you had never stopped to analyze. Writing it all down on paper forces you to think about the problem, and allows your subconscious mind to provide solutions. In the letter you can discuss the problem in detail, weigh up the pros and cons of alternative solutions, and write down all the thoughts that come to you as you write.

Do not concern yourself with a solution as you write. Often, the answer will come while you are still writing, but more frequently the answer will come later, usually when you are thinking about something else entirely.

Even if a solution does not appear right away, the awareness that you gain from this exercise is extremely helpful. You will be able to look at the problem differently, and possibly change your feelings about it. Once you know what you are afraid of, you will be able to make the necessary changes in your attitude and outlook to overcome the problem.

Although it's not magic in the truest sense of the word, writing down your problems and finding a solution is definitely writing your own magic.

Of course, as a child you instinctively knew how magical words could be. You probably remember fairy tales where spells were cast, and good ultimately triumphed. Perhaps you wished that you could cast a spell and achieve your own dreams. You can do this. By the end of this book you will be using the magic of words to write your own magic, cast spells, and achieve your goals.

The Four Magic Steps

Chapter 2

A word is worth a thousand pieces of gold.

CHINESE IDIOM

I AM ASSUMING that you want greater success in your life than you are receiving at the moment. If you were already enjoying all the success you desire, there would be no need to read this book. I am also assuming that you are prepared to do something about your present condition, as even reading this book takes some degree of effort. This means that your desire for a better life is so strong that you are prepared to make whatever changes are necessary to enable it to happen.

Many of these changes are inside you. For instance, you might need to change your attitude towards yourself and others. If you are full of hate, envy, or any other harmful emotion, you will have to release this negativity before you can attain your goals.

Maybe you think many more negative thoughts than positive ones and need to change your way of thinking. As we attract to us what we think about, it is extremely important to stay in control of our thoughts.

Perhaps you need to continue your education to provide the qualifications that are necessary in the field you want to succeed in. You can do this in many ways. It is even possible to take college courses over the Internet. Alternatively, night classes or reading up on the latest trends in your industry may be all that is necessary. Education should be a life-long process.

Not long ago, I read of a highly successful attorney who had initially left school with no qualifications. For several years he lived for the moment. He surfed, drank too much, and dabbled in drugs. One day when he was in his late twenties, he happened to meet someone who had been in his class in school. During the course of the conversation, he discovered that his classmate was now a doctor. This person also told him about other people they had been at school with, and he discovered that they were all doing well with their lives. This made him pause and take stock of his own life. He turned his back on his previous life, returned home, and went to college. It was hard work, but he eventually got a degree. This success inspired him to carry on with his education, and eventually to begin work as an attorney. This man knew what he had to do. He knew he had the ability. And he went out and made it happen. It's interesting to wonder what would have happened to him if he had not accidentally met his former classmate on the street.

You must have a strong desire. Most people are full of conflicting desires. They want this, they want that, but they don't want the other thing. They are like children deciding what they want for Christmas. It is fine to have several different goals, but they must be compatible with each other, and you must fervently desire them.

There are four deceptively simple steps that lead toward the attainment of your desires:

1. Dream what you want.
2. Write the dream down.
3. Tell the universe what you want.
4. Become a magnet that attracts your desires to you.

Frequently, people tell me about dreams that they think might be too ambitious for them to attempt. These people are underestimating themselves. If you have the ability to dream something, you also have the ability to make it happen. In fact, it is usually good to aim for a dream that is so ambitious it frightens you. This gives you an added edge that ultimately demolishes anything that stands in the path of your success.

You have a number of dreams every single night. Usually these dreams are simply fantasies that never come true. To make the dream a reality, you need to follow all four steps listed above. When you write the dream down, you are in effect setting a goal for yourself. A dream normally fades away quickly and is forgotten. Once you write the dream down, you are creating a record that will remind you of its existence every time you see the piece of paper.

In one sense, writing the dream down is telling the universe that you want this particular dream to become a reality. However, you need to do much more than that to ensure that your dream comes true. Consequently, this book contains a number of rituals, ceremonies, and spells to help you send your energies out into the universe.

Finally, you must be prepared to receive what you want. To do this you need to magnetize yourself so that your desires are attracted to you, while at the same time the things that you do not want are repelled.

This may seem too simple to be true. However, it works. I have seen this process transform the lives of many people, including my own. I know how successful the process is, but I do not want you to simply accept what I say. I want you to prove it for yourself.

Barbara was a student at one of my psychic development classes many years ago. She was small and shy and gave a nervous laugh whenever anyone spoke to her. She sat in the back row of the class and took copious notes, but did not speak unless someone asked her a specific question. I always served tea and coffee after these classes, and anyone who wanted could stay and discuss what we had covered that night. Barbara stayed behind on the third week. I could tell she was anxious to say something but lacked the confidence to speak in front of the others. After everyone else had left, she asked me if writing down what she desired would really work.

"Do it," I advised, "and find out for yourself."

Barbara hesitated. "Have you done it?"

I laughed. "Barbara," I said, "just a few years ago these classes were a dream of mine. You wouldn't be here tonight if I hadn't written my dream down."

"So it does work?"

"Let me know when you've proved it for yourself."

After that, Barbara became slightly more outgoing. She stayed every week after class, listened to what the others had to say, and occasionally made a small contribution. When the class finished, I did not expect to see her again.

Much to my surprise, she enrolled for the same basic psychic development class again. I called her to tell her that she had already done this particular class and to suggest some alternatives for her.

"No," she said. "It's working, and I want to do the class again to make sure it happens."

Barbara was noticeably more outgoing the second time she did the class. She was proud of the fact that she already knew the answers to most of the questions I asked, and she frequently volunteered answers. This time she sat in the second row, near the middle, rather than at the back of the room.

She was extremely excited when she arrived for the final session of the course, and asked if she could say something to the class as a whole. I was surprised to hear this, and happily agreed.

"As you know, this is the second time I've done this class," she began, speaking in a surprisingly strong voice. "On the third week of the first class I went home and wrote down what I wanted. I sent it out to the universe and magnetized myself. I want you all to know that it worked." She held up her left hand and proudly displayed a beautiful engagement ring. "I hope you're all writing down your dreams. It works!"

Barbara was rather skeptical when I first explained the concept to her, but she went away and proved it for herself. There is no need to believe in what we are discussing here. Belief does not come into it. All you have to do is do it, and you can make your dreams come true.

Aristotle coined the word *entelechy*, which describes the complete realization of something that was formerly in a potential or undeveloped state. Nature is full of examples of this. A beautiful butterfly coming out of its cocoon is an example. A tiny acorn turning into a majestic oak tree is another. We are all potentially part of this process. I believe that we are all here to achieve something. Once we find out what that something is, our progress can be a joy to behold. By using the ideas in this book to find out what you should be doing with your life, and then going on to achieve it, you will fulfill your purpose in this incarnation.

We'll start on the process in the next chapter.

Big Dreams and Little Dreams

Chapter 3

Whenever you are fed up with life, start writing: ink is the great cure for all human ills, as I have found out long ago.

C. S. LEWIS (1898–1963)

WE ALL HAVE HOPES AND DREAMS, and the purpose of this book is to enable you to turn your hopes and dreams into reality. There is no limit to what you can ask for. For instance, you might want one or many of the following:

vibrant health
a fulfilling relationship
more money
more friends
greater confidence
increased happiness
a better job
your own business
an overseas vacation
a stronger faith
greater intuition
a date on Saturday night

All of these, and much more, can be brought into your life when you write your own magic.

Manifesting Your Dreams

The basic concept is simple. All you have to do is decide what you want, write it down, send the desire out into the universe, and wait for it to happen. In practice, though, there are a few provisos.

The most important proviso is that your dreams hurt no one else. Naturally, most of your dreams will be for your own benefit, but you must ensure that no one will be hurt in the process. If, for example, your dream is to free yourself from a restrictive relationship, you should not wish any harm on the other person, no matter what that person may have done to you in the past. Wish for the relationship to end, by all means, but phrase the request in such a way that no one gets hurt. We will discuss how to phrase our requests in chapter 5.

Wishing evil or harm on anyone else is black magic. You can use these techniques to hurt others, but the law of karma will then come into play, and you will ultimately suffer at least as much as the person you have harmed. We all reap what we sow. If you do a good deed, sooner or later something good will come back to you. Likewise, if you do a bad deed, sooner or later you will be made to pay for it. The law of karma is completely impartial.

White magic is good magic. If you use these techniques for good, you, and everyone your life touches, will benefit. Good intentions produce good results; evil intentions create more evil. If you use the universal forces of love, kindness, and compassion when deciding what to ask for, you will always receive rich rewards.

Recently, I had to explain to a young woman who was using magic to attract a certain young man to her that what she was doing was black magic. She found this hard to understand, as she was bringing in to her life what she wanted. However, she was completely ignoring the needs or desires of the young man. She did not care what his desires were, and this is what made it black magic. It is important to look at all sides of a situation before using magic.

You also need to ask other people's permission before using magic on them, even if your magic is intended to help them. They may not need or want your help. It may seem strange that someone who is seriously ill, for instance, may not want you to use magic to help them.

I have a classic example of this. A woman I knew became extremely ill after the death of her husband. Doctors could find nothing wrong with her, and were puzzled as she gradually faded away and ultimately died. She had lost the will to live after her soul mate died, and effectively caused her own death. The last thing she wanted was to have someone trying to effect a cure. Consequently, make sure that you ask other people before using magic on them.

Some people feel that all of their requests are selfish. One lady told me that all she ever seemed to ask for was pretty clothes and good-looking partners. There is nothing wrong with asking for things that make you feel good. When this lady was wearing beautiful clothes and was walking arm-in-arm with an attractive man, she felt vibrant and more fully alive than at any other time. It also proved to her how effective writing her own magic was.

In practice, I have found that most people start out by asking for what may be considered selfish or superficial requests. However, over a period of time the nature of their requests change, and almost invariably the serious searchers start seeking greater spiritual growth.

You can ask for anything at all, just as long as your request hurts no one else.

Finding Your Life's Purpose

Many people are happy asking for anything they happen to desire at the time. However, once they write their own magic and see the amazing results that can be gained, most people become interested in using this system to help them achieve their life's purpose.

Many people find this hard to do. This is because few people have a clear idea of what they want out of life. Some people are extremely fortunate and decide at an early age what they are going to do with the rest of their lives. Most people, though, drift all over the place, with no clear goals or purpose.

If you already know what it is that you want, you can move on to chapter 5. However, if you are like most people, you should give serious attention to what it is you really want to achieve in this lifetime.

What did you come into this life to do? How do you want to be remembered once you are dead and gone? Most people tend to avoid questions like this. Deep down they are aware that they are here for some purpose, but choose not to think about it.

The first step is to allow some time for yourself, so that you can think back over your life. I usually go for a long walk in the country whenever I do this exercise. This takes me away from home and any interruptions, and gives me time to be on my own. You may prefer to sit down quietly at home, just as long as you will not be disturbed for the length of time you set.

Allow your mind to drift back over your life, beginning in early childhood. We all had hopes and dreams when we were very young. Obviously, some of them are childish dreams that have no relevance now, but some of them may give a clue to what you really desire. What did you really enjoy doing as a youngster?

As a child I wanted to be a writer. I wrote all the time, and at one stage had a small newspaper that I sold to my neighbors. When I left school I went into publishing, thinking that this would give me valuable insights into the world of books and writing. I never gave up writing, but gradually the idea of becoming a full-time writer faded away, and I became involved in a variety of other activities. It was only when I deliberately went on a long walk to decide what I really wanted to do that the possibility of becoming a writer came back to me. It was a childhood dream that had always been at the back of my mind, but I had to do this exercise to make it a possibility.

Incidentally, as a child I also wanted to become a magician, hypnotist, and musician, and I have done all of these things professionally as an adult. However, these ambitions were never as strong as my desire to write. If your quiet time produces several goals, evaluate them carefully and choose the most important one to work on first. In time, you may want to manifest all of these different goals, but it is best to focus on one of them at a time.

You may find that your childhood years give no indication as to what you should be doing. In this case, keep gradually moving forward through your life. Think about the people you admired, occupations and activities that you found interesting, important hobbies, and anything else that attracted your attention. Think about what your friends and acquaintances are doing, and see if their activities can provide insights into what you should be doing.

It is possible that you will go through your entire life and still have no idea as to what it is you want to do. Large numbers of people live their entire lives this way. Fortunately, you are different. You may have no idea now, but by following the ideas in this chapter, you soon will.

Your Five-Year Plan

Sit down with pen and paper and think about what you would like your life to be like five years from now. Write down everything that occurs to you. Naturally, you will probably want to be better off financially than you are now. If so, write it down. Think about the home you are living in. Do you still want to be living in the same place five years from now? If not, write down the sort of home you would like to be living in five years from now. What other changes would you like? More friends, perhaps? A life partner, or children? Would you like to be doing the same work you are doing now in five years' time? If not, think about what job you would like to be doing. While you are doing this exercise, think about the things that you enjoy doing, and write them down as well.

Write down whatever occurs to you. There are no right or wrong answers, and no one will see what you have written down unless you show it to them.

Maybe the job you would like to be doing requires you to further your education, or gain additional work experience. Are you prepared to do whatever is necessary to ensure that you have the right qualifications for the job you want to do? There is always a price to be paid. If the price seems to be too high, cross out that particular idea. You will never achieve that goal if you are not prepared to pay the price. This is why it is so important to choose a goal that is right for you.

Two runners I knew at school illustrate a good example of this. Initially, they were roughly equal in ability. One took athletics seriously and trained regularly. The other simply relied on his natural ability. Within a year, the one who trained was competing in championships all over the state, while the other took part only in high-school events. The first one was prepared to pay the price, but the other was not.

Finally, there is something else you can do if going over your life and thinking about five years from now has not provided you with a worthwhile goal. Read out loud everything you have written down about the life you want to be leading five years from now immediately before going to sleep. This means that you will drift off to sleep thinking about the wonderful life you will be leading a few years from now. During the night your subconscious mind will work on this information, and will pass on ideas to you. Write down any insights that come to you as soon as they occur. If you do not do this immediately, some of them will be lost. Read your notes out loud every night until you have a clear goal to work toward. Be patient. If you have never deliberately set a goal for yourself before, it might take time. Remain confident that it will come to you when it is ready.

The Six-Sided Person

While you are thinking about your life's purpose, you need to remember that you are a multidimensional being. You may think that having a million dollars in the bank is all you need for long-term happiness, but a few moments of reflection will show that this is most unlikely. It would be an extremely rare and unusual person who would be totally happy all of the time simply for having plenty of money in the bank.

Naturally, you need to make financial goals for yourself. However, you also need long-term goals for all of the other areas of your life. What do you want to achieve mentally, physically, socially, and spiritually? Do you want to develop your intuitive awareness? These are all just as important as financial goals.

They all work together, also. What use would all the money in the world be if you were suffering from a fatal illness? What would be the benefit of a powerful intellect if you found yourself unable to mix and have fun with other human beings? What use would a magnificent physique be if you were a spiritual dwarf? Could you use your magnificent brain to its fullest ability if you totally ignored your intuition?

Ideally, you should set goals to develop all six areas of your life. Each area helps every other area to make a complete whole. As you embark on a program of learning, you will have more to talk about with others, and your income is likely to improve. As you become physically fitter, you will have more energy and zest for life. This creates enthusiasm, which in turn helps every other area. As you develop spiritually and intuitively, you become more aware of your place in the scheme of things. You become more self-accepting. You will worry less and take life more as it comes.

In the next chapter we will discuss different ideas to help you decide what to ask for.

How to Determine What to Ask For

Chapter 4

For words, like Nature, half reveal and half conceal the Soul within.

ALFRED LORD TENNYSON (1809–1892)

THERE IS NO LIMIT to the type or number of requests you can make. By writing your own magic you can attain anything you wish, as long as your requests are sincere and hurt no one. Of course, you must also perform the ritual sincerely, and remain patient until your request is granted.

We all have hopes and dreams. Some of these are just passing fancies, and we are not prepared to do whatever it would take to attain them. Others are much more important.

I find it helpful to sit down and write out a list of everything I want. Some of these are purely personal, even selfish, desires. Others are intended to help others, especially the people I love and care about. Until I have made up a list I have no clear idea as to what it is that I want. Once the list has been drawn up, I put it aside for a few days. During that time various ideas will come into my mind, and I will probably add a few things to the list. I may even remove something if I decide that it is not what I want after all.

Once I have completed this, I look at the list again and decide which requests are the most important. I will work on them first and gradually move on to the less important ones.

This procedure is a simple one in theory, but many people have problems deciding what it is they want. Naturally, most people want more money and peace in the world, but we need to be much more specific than this before sending our request out into the universe.

There are three methods that I have found extremely useful for determining and clarifying your requests: keeping a magical diary, automatic writing, and writing a letter to your guardian angel.

Your Magical Diary

A magical diary is in many ways a normal diary. However, you need not write in it every day. It is intended to be a record of your thoughts, reflections, and feelings. You can use it as a normal diary as well, and include a record of what you did each day if you wish. There are no hard-and-fast rules.

I find a hard-covered exercise book to be more suitable than a commercially available diary. The problem with commercial products is that you have a set amount of space for each day. With a magical diary you may not want to write every day, and then, when you do write, it might be a few lines one day and five pages the next. Choose a book that looks attractive to you. You will be using it regularly and writing your innermost thoughts in it. The book will become your friend, and you want it to be aesthetically pleasing. You may want to decorate it in some way, or design a cover for it. It does not matter what you do. It is your private book and you can do whatever you want with it.

You may prefer a book that is unlined. I prefer to have lines in my diary and choose books that have three lines to the inch. This suits my writing and I can write easily, without feeling restricted in any way. You may prefer a book that has two or four lines to the inch. Again, it is entirely up to you.

Write in your magical diary whenever you feel like it. At first it may feel strange sitting down and writing your innermost thoughts. Many people's diaries start out in a stilted manner and become freer as they gradually become comfortable with the process. It is important that you are the only person to read your diary. If you feel that it might be read by others, you are likely to censor what you write. Lock your diary away if necessary, and keep the key on you at all times.

You may set aside a certain time to write in your diary. I usually write in mine as the family is preparing for bed. This gives me a quiet time in which to reflect on the day. However, I have met several people who carry their diaries around with them and insert brief thoughts as and when they occur to them during the day. Again, whatever method suits you is fine.

What you choose to record is up to you also. You might like to record your dreams in it. Your diary may consist solely of the results of your soul-searching. It may contain an account of your daily life in great detail, including remembered conversations.

You should include your hopes and desires, as these may well become future requests.

The important thing is to be as honest as possible. If you had an argument with someone and came off second-best, record that in your diary. Do not edit or change it to make the incident appear better than it was. If you are going to record it, write it down exactly as it happened.

Simply write in your diary what occurs to you. In time your diary will become your confidante, your best friend. You will be able to write in it things that you may never have told anyone else.

What is the point of all this? After you have kept your diary for a while, you will notice that certain themes and ideas will come up again and again. By thinking about these, you will gain insight as to the requests you should make to the universe.

Use your diary to record all your requests. You should clearly date every entry in your diary. I even write down the time of day I start and finish writing. By clearly recording your requests in this way, you will know how long it takes each one to be granted. Naturally, you should record this information as well. Sometimes requests will be granted in a manner or form that you did not expect. Record this information also.

As time goes by your diary will become more and more valuable to you. It will provide a record of your successes and disappointments, as well as your growth and development.

Automatic Writing

Automatic writing is a method of communication that works through you, rather than by you. Although you use pen and paper, the pen is directed by some power other than your conscious mind. Complete books have been written using automatic writing. *Private Dowding*, transcribed by W. T. Poole, is a good example of a book written this way. Thomas Dowding was a young English school teacher who was killed by shrapnel during the First World War. This book became a bestseller in 1918 and gave hope to many people who had lost their sons during the war, because it provided hope that death was not the end.

Anyone can learn to do automatic writing, but like anything else, it takes practice. Start by sitting comfortably with a pen in your writing hand resting on a sheet of paper. This arm should be bent at a right angle at the elbow. It is worth noting that some people receive better results when using the opposite hand to the one they normally use for writing.

Relax as much as you can and simply wait to see what happens. You may wish to close your eyes, but this is not essential.

After a while the hand that is holding the pen will start to move. Pay no attention to this. This is unconscious writing and the flow will stop as soon as you give it your conscious attention.

Most people start by drawing shapes that are not related to anything. A few people start by drawing words and sentences. A few even write sentences in mirror writing. Do not be concerned about what you produce when you first start. Any movement of the pen is good, and the more you practice, the better you will become. You will quickly discover that any involvement by your conscious mind will stop the flow of writing. Many people find the hardest part of automatic writing is letting go of their conscious mind, so that the subconscious is allowed free reign.

Remember that there may not always be any information to come through. Consequently, even after you are receiving good results on a regular basis, you will encounter occasions when the pen will not move at all.

Automatic writing is called this for a good reason. The writing is totally automatic, and sometimes the speed of the writing can be amazing. You will be able to write for hours on end without feeling tired.

Once you become experienced at automatic writing you will be amazed at what you produce. You may write poems or novels, receive answers to questions that are bothering you, gain spiritual insights, or ideas for the future direction of your life. Once you know what these are, it is a simple matter to send them out into the universe, and make them manifest in your life.

You are not limited to words, either. Drawings, paintings, and music have all been created with automatic writing. Rosemary Brown, a British widow who is in touch with the spirits of many composers including Bach, Beethoven, Brahms, Chopin, Mozart, and

Schubert, has produced music in their styles all through automatic writing.

You will be in good company if you practice automatic writing. Alfred Lord Tennyson, William Butler Yeats, and Gertrude Stein are just a few of the authors who have experimented with this to help their creativity.

It takes time to become proficient at automatic writing, but it is worth persevering as the results can be incredible. You will find it a useful tool in every part of your life.

Writing to Your Guardian Angel

The concept of a personal guardian angel who looks after us dates back some two thousand years. Around 150 C.E. a man called Hermas wrote down his experiences with his personal guardian angel. His book *Shepherd of Hermas* became extremely popular as it encouraged people to consider angels as their own personal shepherds of God.[1] There are two important quotations from the Bible that give credence to the idea of guardian angels: "He will give his angels charge of you, to guard you in all your ways,"[2] and "Take heed that ye despise not one of these little ones, for I say unto you, That in heaven their angels do always behold the face of my Father which is in heaven."[3]

Carl Jung, a lifelong believer in angels, wrote in his autobiography that angels "are soulless beings who represent nothing but the thoughts and intuitions of their Lord."[4] Consequently, when you write a letter to your guardian angel, you are, in effect, writing a letter to God.

Interestingly enough, writing a letter to your guardian angel works, regardless of your personal beliefs about angels. If you do not accept the concept of a personal guardian angel, write a letter to someone who you revere. You might write a letter to Buddha, or one of the saints. You might even write to a famous person in history whom you particularly admire.

More important than your choice of person is the knowledge that you are writing to someone who you believe can help. This person is sacred, holy, or special to you in some way. Consequently, the letter you write will be different from a letter you would send to a friend or relative. Your guardian angel (or whomever you write to) already knows everything about you, so you can write openly and honestly.

Start by writing about yourself, your home, and loved ones. Write about your hopes and fears. Tell your guardian angel about anything in your life that is not going as well as you would like it to be. Write about your frustrations and difficulties. Write about your successes.

You are not likely to write a letter like this in one sitting. Spread the writing over several days, as this gives your subconscious mind an opportunity to think about what it would like you to write down. Something that might not occur to you on Monday may well be extremely important on Friday. Simply write everything down as it occurs to you.

Once you have completed the letter, place it in an envelope and address it to your guardian angel (or whomever it is you have written to). Put it aside for at least three days, preferably longer. After this time, open the letter and read it with a highlighter pen in your hand. The purpose of allowing at least a few days between writing the letter and reading it is to ensure that you read it with fresh eyes. Highlight anything that seems important to you as you read the letter. You may find that by the end you have high-lighted virtually the entire letter. You may find that you highlight very little. It makes no difference. The parts that you have highlighted are the areas that you need to focus on. Devise requests that relate to them and send them out into the universe.

In practice, once you start writing your own magic, you will have few problems knowing what to request. Ideas will come to you all the time, and you will prob-ably have to pick and choose, rather than search for, a specific request.

Write It Down

Chapter 5

The moving finger writes; and having writ,
Moves on: not all thy piety nor wit
Shall lure it back to cancel half a line,
Nor all thy tears wash out a word of it.

RUBÁIYÁT OF OMAR KHAYYÁM (C.1050–C.1122)
(TRANSLATED BY EDWARD FITZGERALD)

BY FOLLOWING THE EXERCISES in the previous chapter you will have a number of ideas about what you want. At the moment, these are simply dreams. What you need to do now is look at them one at a time and turn them into goals, complete with a plan of action as to how you are going to achieve them.

It is a good idea to have a notebook to record all your ideas and dreams in. Write down everything that occurs to you, no matter how unusual or far-fetched it may seem. Something that seems totally impossible today, may be easy to achieve six months from now. However, if you do not write it down, the thought is likely to disappear and never be realized.

Evaluate your ideas and categorize them into the six areas of your life: financial, mental, physical, social, spiritual, and intuitive. Number these ideas by degree of importance. Usually, the most important idea is the best one to start with. However, if this particular dream will take years to realize, start with another idea that you can achieve in the next few months. This is because achieving this goal will prove to you that the system works and encourage you to carry on with your longer-term goals.

It is important that your goal be as specific as possible. Many people set goals that are far too vague. They say, for instance, that they want to be rich, or happy, or married. These are worthy aims, but they do not constitute a worthwhile goal by themselves. They make a good start toward setting a goal, and the true goal can be found by asking questions.

If, for instance, your goal is to become rich, there are several questions that you can ask yourself. Just how rich do you want to be? Write down the specific amount of money you want to have. What will you do to make this amount of money? Is this something that you will enjoy doing? It is not easy to make money, and you will find it extremely hard to make a great deal of money doing something that you hate. How long will it take to make this amount of money? How will your life be different once you have this amount of money? Will making this amount of money make you happy? What will you do once you have this money? Writing down the answers to these, and any other questions that occur to you, will help you clarify your thoughts. They will also reveal the price you will have to pay to achieve your goal. There is always a price that needs to be paid.

It is important to write down the answers to all these questions. Once you have them recorded in your notebook you can then rewrite the main points as a goal. Someone who wants to become rich, for instance, might end up with the following goal: "I intend to make one million dollars by owning and operating my own pizza restaurant. I intend to create my own distinctive recipes to make my pizzas different—and better—than anything else on the market. I will do this in the next ten years. Once I have made one million dollars, I will buy my dream home on the east side and be able to devote at least a third of my time to helping people less fortunate than myself. Signed, John Smith."

This goal is clear and specific. John intends to make a million dollars in ten years. He knows how he is going to do it. He also knows what he is going to do with the money, once he has it. However, this is only part of John's ultimate goal. To make it complete, he needs to look at the other five areas of his life and work out similar goals for each of them.

Here is another example. Doreen has been divorced for several years and is tired of living on her own. She wants to find a new boyfriend. She may write down: "I am going to find a new partner for myself. He will be at least six feet tall, and be somewhere between thirty-five and forty years old. He will be a good conversationalist and we will have interests in common. To help find him, I will accept every opportunity that comes my way to meet new people. I will also start taking dancing lessons again."

Doreen has been reasonably specific about the sort of man she wants. She also has a plan of action (accepting every opportunity to meet people), as she realizes that she will never meet anyone if she stays at home in her apartment. Writing all of this information down forces Doreen to think carefully about what it is she really wants. She has not asked simply for a man, she wants a particular man (a good conversationalist who is over six feet tall and between the ages of thirty-five and forty).

She could have been much more specific than this if she wanted. She could have specified eye and hair color, education level, occupation, income level, degree of athleticism, and so on. However, by not mentioning these factors, she has provided an opportunity for a larger selection of men to come into her life. Naturally, like John Smith, Doreen will also have to work out plans for the other areas of her life.

Here is a more complete life plan. Joshua has worked out a life goal for himself: "I intend to succeed as a composer and create memorable music that people of all ages will enjoy. I intend to earn $100,000 a year from my music. To do this, I will compose, record, and perform until composing on its own earns me this sum each year. I will find a permanent gig in a restaurant within the next three months. This will provide both a regular income, but also a venue where I can play my own compositions. In the next six months I will find three talented musicians to form a group that will play mainly my own work. I aim to have a recording contract for this group within the next eighteen months. Ultimately, I want to be able to support myself and my family from my compositions, and then be free to play professionally as and when I wish, rather than by financial necessity. I intend this to be the case five years from now. I have no plans to retire as I love what I do. I want my music to be played long after my death, and I want my children to have the benefit of the royalties to help them become established in their respective fields.

"I intend to return to the university and complete my music degree. I estimate that this will take three years, as I am going to be extremely busy and will have little time for study. However, it is important to me to attain these qualifications. I will derive enormous satisfaction from completing my degree, and it will also give me increased credibility in my field.

"My work will increase my circle of acquaintances and friends. I find it easy to make friends anyway, but the more people I get to know the better, as much of my work revolves around contacts. I also enjoy hearing many different points of view, and a wider circle of friends will expose me to many more viewpoints.

"Being with my family is the most important part of my life. They are my whole reason for being, and none of my goals would be worth pursuing if it wasn't for them. Consequently, although my career is important, I will not allow it to take precedence over my home and family life. This may cost me opportunities, but I am not prepared to sacrifice my loved ones for the sake of my career.

"I will join a gym in the next few days. I am aware that I am not as physically fit as I used to be. It is important to me to have the necessary stamina and energy to achieve my goals, and physical fitness is essential.

"My faith is developing slowly, and I intend to put more effort into this area of my life. Over the next six months, I resolve to explore all the channels of spirituality that I can find, and to increase my knowledge in this area by reading at least twenty books. I am sure that my creativity will increase rapidly once I open myself up to my creator. I feel that I am reasonably intuitive, and I will keep a notebook to record all of my premonitions, and anything else that comes from my intuitive mind."

Joshua obviously wants to write music that lasts long after his death. He has created, in effect, a series of small goals that lead to his ultimate aim of earning a comfortable six-figure income from composing alone. However, he has not forgotten the other areas of his life, and has set goals for himself for each of these. Joshua may think that he has completed a life plan for himself, but nothing in his plan, except for his ultimate goal, extends more than five years into the future. At some stage, he will have to revise and modify his plan. This is good. Our lives are never static, and something that is important to us now, may be of no account in the future. Our plans should always be flexible, and we should not hesitate to change them when it feels right to do so.

A good example of this is a school friend of mine who became a successful attorney. However, in his late thirties, to everyone's amazement, he bought a farm and has been blissfully happy ever since. He freely admits that the career change was as much a surprise to him as to everyone else. One of his clients happened to mention that he was selling his farm and my friend expressed interest. Two months later, he had given up his law practice and was learning to become a farmer.

The universe can sometimes put surprising situations in our paths, and we must be flexible enough to seize the good opportunities. Naturally, if you take advantage of something like this, you will need to set new goals for yourself.

The next stage is to send our desires out into the universe. We will start discussing this in the next chapter.

Making Magic

Chapter 6

Do you really believe that the sciences would ever have originated and grown if the way had not been prepared by magicians, alchemists, astrologers, and witches whose promises and pretensions first had to create a thirst, a hunger, a taste for hidden and forbidden powers?

FRIEDRICH WILHELM NIETZSCHE (1844–1900)

THERE HAS ALWAYS BEEN MAGIC, and there always will be. Just think about your own life for a moment. Wasn't there something magical about the first time you fell in love? Have you ever watched a perfect sunset, or gazed up at the stars on a beautiful evening? Have you ever listened to a piece of music that stirred your soul? Have you ever watched a toddler's first trembling steps, or watched a bird feed its young? At one time we had two young kittens and I spent countless hours watching them play together. For me, that was magic. Magic is all around us, and the tragedy is that so few people actually recognize it for what it is.

All creativity is magic, and despite what you may think, you are highly creative. Every time you have a thought you are creating something—and that is highly magical.

Magic is based on the realization that everything in the world is interrelated. When performing magic, a number of things occur. First, you enter a heightened state of awareness in which magic can occur. You become totally focused on your desire or goal. Additionally, you follow a set order of events each time you perform a ritual or cast a spell. All of this allows the magic to happen.

People have used the forces of nature to influence the course of events from ancient times. It is believed that magic may have started in India and then spread around the globe, but there is no proof of this. There is evidence of early magical activity dating from the Middle Paleolithic age in many caves in Europe, particularly in the Aurignac region in France.[1]

The ancient Egyptians and Babylonians had well-developed magical systems, and many of their teachings were incorporated into the magic of Greece and Rome. The three kings or wise men who came to visit the infant Jesus were magi, or magicians. Moses and Solomon were also magicians.

Unfortunately, after this golden period the early church forced magic underground, but it never entirely disappeared. Medieval magic began to take shape in the twelfth century, and was probably introduced to Europe by soldiers returning from the Crusades. It reached its greatest heights with the work of Paracelsus and Cornelius Agrippa, who were the most notable magicians of the Middle Ages.

Many famous and influential people throughout history have practiced the magical arts. Pythagoras, Leonardo da Vinci, and Isaac Newton are good examples. William Shakespeare made countless references to magic in his plays, and was obviously familiar with the subject.

Magic can be divided into two categories: exoteric and esoteric. Exoteric magic was taught openly and consists of legends, pictures, and symbols, such as can be found in *The Arabian Nights*, many fairy tales, and some Bible stories. Esoteric magic was secret, and was usually transmitted by word of mouth from generation to generation. Esoteric magic provides the necessary insight to fully understand the pretty pictures of exoteric magic. Secrecy—as in "Know, dare, will, and keep silent"—was of prime importance.

Much of the Bible was written in esoteric form. The famous theosophist Geoffrey Hodson wrote in his mammoth four-volume work *The Hidden Wisdom in the Holy Bible:* "These allegories are said to preserve for posterity, to reveal, and yet to conceal profound spiritual and therefore power-bestowing truths."[2] In the *Clementine Homilies,* written in Rome about 95 C.E., we read: "And Peter said, 'We remember that our Lord and Teacher commanding us said "Guard the Mysteries for me and the sons of my house."' Wherefore also he explained to his disciples privately the Mysteries of the Kingdom of the Heavens."[3]

The hidden teachings were revealed only to the initiated. Polycrap, Bishop of Smyrna, was obviously not included in this select group when he wrote to the Philippians: "For I trust that ye are well versed in the sacred Scriptures and that nothing is hid from you, but to me this privilege is not yet granted."[4] Large parts of the Scriptures were written in a concealed form, which can be described as esoteric magic. The authors were deliberately writing their own magic.

When we use magic we tune into the forces of nature. We use the universal energy that is present in everything. This creative energy connects and joins everything in the universe. Although we may think that we are completely separate from each other and everything else in the universe, in reality we are all connected.

Throughout history, universal energy has been known by different names. Spirit, God, ch'i, and prana are examples. Universal energy is being created all the time. Every time you have a thought you are creating universal energy. Idle thoughts create little energy, but directed thoughts have the power to change the world. Prayers, affirmations, goals, and magic all create large amounts of universal energy. This universal energy cannot be destroyed but it can be guided and transformed, which is exactly what we do when we write our own magic.

Aleister Crowley, a famous early twentieth-century magician and author, defined magic as "the Science and Art of causing Change to occur in conformity with Will."⁵ Florence Farr, one of the leading members of the Golden Dawn, defined it this way: "Magic consists of removing the limitations from what we think are the earthly and spiritual laws that bind or compel us. We can be anything because we are All."⁶ A simpler definition would be to say that magic is the art of attracting to you what you want.

Obviously, we have to know what we want before performing magic. We must also have intention. We need to know what we want, but it is best if we allow the universe to manifest it in the form that it decides. You may have a strong desire to be promoted at work. You may have the exact position you want firmly planted in your mind. However, if you become too fixed in this specific outcome, you may lose the possibility of a better result. Have a strong intent, but do not try to force a specific outcome. In the above example, sending out a request for a better position may create a better job in another company, or an even better promotion at work than the one you had set your mind upon. You need to allow the magic to happen in its own way, without trying to influence the outcome.

In Persia, the magi were a class of priests. The word *magic* came into our vocabulary from the Greek, which had previously adopted it from Persian. It may be related to the word *magikos*, which means "power of the magicians," or perhaps *megas*, which means "great." It may even have come from *magein*, the philosophy and beliefs of the priests of Zoroaster.

When you create a ritual and send your desire or goal out into the universe you are creating magic. You are using the natural laws or forces of nature to attain your particular goal. Ideally, this goal will enrich you, the people around you, and your environment. By doing this, you are taking positive steps to control your own life, and your personal growth and development will speed up immensely. You will find it rewarding, satisfying, and fulfilling. In the process

you will discover that you really can attain anything
that you desire.

Ritual

A ritual is a procedure, or a way of conducting a ceremony, that enables you to achieve your dreams. Its
purpose is to create the desired environment in which
magic will occur, and consequently bring benefits to
the life of whoever is conducting the ritual. A ritual
should never be performed frivolously.

Ritual is a common practice in organized religion.
Both magic and religion recognize the cosmic forces
that shape our destinies. When we pray, we do so
believing that the cosmic forces will answer our
prayers. When we perform a magic ritual, we also
expect the cosmic forces to provide us with whatever
we ask for.

Ritual itself has enormous power, as it stimulates
and energizes the cosmic forces enabling the magic to
occur. Ritual also stimulates and energizes the person
conducting it by removing all doubt and negativity,
and providing enormous power and personal magnet-
ism. This is why people appear totally transformed
after participating in a ritual.

Some people believe that a ritual is something that
is only performed in a church. However, we are all
performing small rituals all the time. Every morning,
when my son sits down at the breakfast table, he

places everything he is likely to need in a semicircle around his plate before he starts to eat. Everything has a special, set position where it is placed every morning. You could describe what he does as a ritual before eating. You are likely to perform a ritual every morning, also, if you have a set way of getting ready for the day.

In the next chapter we will perform a ritual to enable you to send your desires out into the universe.

Out into the Universe

Chapter 7

My words fly up, my thoughts remain below.
Words without thoughts never to heaven go.

WILLIAM SHAKESPEARE (1564–1616)

YOU HAVE WRITTEN DOWN exactly what you want. Now it is time to perform a·ritual or ceremony to send it out into the universe, confident that your desires will be granted. There are many ways of doing this.

I will start with the method that I was taught originally, and then move on to some other alternatives, all of which I have used at different times. You may ask why I do not stay with one method. It is not easy to answer this. Some requests that I make seem to require a more formal approach to the universe than others. Sometimes I enjoy the ritual and ceremony involved. At other times, the exact moment of asking coincides with a particular time of year (Imbolc, Halloween, etc.) and I might include my request as part of my activities. Finally, sometimes I simply prefer a "quick and easy" request, while on other occasions I prefer to make my request more slowly. What I do at any particular time depends on the time of year, how I am feeling, how much time I have available, and what seems right for the particular desire I have.

There are a number of factors that need to be in place before you send your desire out into the universe: your environment, posture, and clothing.

The Best Places in Which to Work

Naturally, the best place is anywhere where you will not be disturbed. It needs to be quiet, comfortable, and away from any distractions. If you live on your own, this may well be your living room. If other people live with you, it may be better to do this in your bedroom, or another room where you are unlikely to be disturbed. If the weather is mild, you may prefer to do this outside, again in a place where you will not be disturbed by other people or extraneous noise. In practice, I usually work outdoors in the summer, but use my home office in the winter.

Make the place suitable for what you are going to do. If you are doing this indoors, tidy up the room and remove from sight anything that might prove distracting later on. Make the room as sacred as possible. You may have a picture you can display, for instance. You may wish to place four white candles at the north, south, east, and west positions of either your work space or the area you are working in. Alternatively, you might sprinkle a small amount of salt water in these directions.

If you are working outdoors, see if you can site yourself close a friendly, protective tree. The druids called these *oracle trees*.[1] You can find your own particular tree by hugging trees until you find one that responds to you. Do not hug every tree in sight; choose trees that appeal to you aesthetically. I find older trees seem to respond better than young ones. It pays to experiment. You may find a younger tree that responds perfectly to you.

Once you have found your tree, clean up the area around it. This is a necessary preparation before sending your desire out into the universe, and it helps create a strong bond between you and your oracle tree.

Some people have a special rug to work on. This is fine, as it denotes a special area to work within. However, do not allow yourself to feel restricted to a particular area. If, for example, you are doing a walking meditation (to be explained shortly) you will need plenty of room in which to complete the ritual.

You may like to have an altar to work on. This can be a designated table that is used only for such purposes, or you may clear a table or shelf when necessary and use it when you are performing a ritual or casting a spell.

Posture

Naturally, you need to be comfortable. The person who taught me insisted on using the lotus position, but I found this to be extremely uncomfortable after a few minutes. There are no set rules about your body position, but it is usually better not to lie down. This is because you may fall asleep before sending your desires out into the universe. If I am outdoors, I usually kneel with my buttocks resting on the back of my legs. Indoors, I either kneel or sit in a straight-backed chair with the backs of my hands resting on my thighs. I always begin this exercise with a meditation and find that I can do this easily and comfortably while in these positions.

Choose a position that is comfortable for you. As you need to be relaxed and free of stress and tension, it is important to be as comfortable as possible. Use pillows and anything else that ensures your comfort.

Clothing

Whatever you wear should be loose and comfortable. Restrictive clothing makes it hard to relax. I have done a number of rituals while wearing a suit, but I always loosened my tie and took off my shoes before starting. Many people have a special loose-fitting robe that they wear for exercises of this sort. If you do this, obtain one that is made of natural fibers.

Some people prefer to send out their desires sky-clad (naked). Obviously, privacy and warmth are essential for this. Taking off your clothes means that you are symbolically removing your normal, everyday persona and releasing the real you. There is some disagreement about the use of jewelry. Some people have special jewelry that they wear only when taking part in magic experiments. Other people take off all of their jewelry before starting. If you work skyclad, it is better to remove all jewelry, as well as your clothes.

Although it may not always be possible, it is beneficial to have a bath or shower before starting. This is particularly important if you are asking for something that relates to long-term personal goals.

You are now ready to begin. Sending your desires out into the universe involves three steps:

1. Relaxation and meditation (about ten minutes)
2. Mantra recitation (about five minutes)
3. Sending out your desire (one to five minutes)

Relaxation and Meditation

The first stage is to relax yourself as much as possible. Ensure that you will not be disturbed for at least half an hour, preferably longer. If you are doing this indoors, you should temporarily disconnect the phone.

You may want to play gentle meditation-type music to help you relax. There is nothing wrong with this, as long as the music contains no recognizable tunes. You do not want to find yourself humming along with the music rather than sending your desires out into the universe. If you choose New Age music, make sure that it does not contain the sound of running water. Music of this sort often contains the sounds of nature, including trickling brooks, ocean waves, and waterfalls. The sound of running water can create a desire to visit the bathroom. Avoid any potential distractions of this sort.

Make sure that the location is warm enough. You may wish to cover yourself with a blanket if you feel cool. Make yourself as comfortable as you can.

There is much misconception about meditation. Meditation is simply a matter of relaxing the body and mind to create a state of peaceful serenity. This may sound easy to do, but it usually takes a great deal of practice to be able to relax both the mind and the body in order to meditate for any length of time. We all become distracted with stray thoughts that unexpectedly come into our minds. Outside influences such as a fly landing on exposed skin, or a sudden sound from another room, can also take your mind off the meditation. While in a meditative state your metabolism, breathing, and heartbeat all slow down. Your brainwaves move from the beta state, which is your normal state of consciousness, to the more peaceful alpha state, thereby revealing an altered state of consciousness.

Of course, although it is pleasant and beneficial to relax your mind and body in this way, this is not true meditation. There is much more to it than that. The ultimate aim is to achieve total mindfulness. When this stage is reached, enlightenment can occur. Consequently, it is a misconception to think that meditation is simply another method of self-development. It is much more than that. True meditation places you in direct contact with the universal forces and enables you to grow in knowledge and wisdom. It provides serenity of mind and opportunities for spiritual growth. It also creates the perfect opportunity for you to request from the universe whatever it is you want.

There are countless ways to meditate. The following is the method I usually use. Sit upright in a comfortable chair with both feet flat on the floor and your spine in an erect position. I use a dining-room type chair for this. You may initially feel more comfortable in an armchair, but in this position your spine will be curved and you will not be able to meditate for long without becoming uncomfortable. A chair with a straight back enables you to remain in a meditative state for as long as you wish without any discomfort.

I like to rest my hands in my lap, palms facing upward, with the right hand resting on the left palm, and with the tips of both thumbs touching each other. Many people prefer to meditate with their hands resting on their thighs.

You can also meditate lying on your back if you wish. I prefer to meditate while lying on the floor, rather than in bed. This is because I am inclined to fall asleep while meditating in bed.

Make yourself comfortable and close your eyes. Take three deep breaths. Count silently and slowly from one to four as you inhale, count to four again as you hold the breath, and then exhale slowly to the count of eight.

Once you have taken three breaths, forget about the counting but continue breathing slowly and deeply. Imagine a wave of relaxation slowly spreading over your entire body, from the top of your head down to the tips of your toes. Feel the relaxation enter every part of your body as it slowly drifts downward.

There is no need to hurry this process. Simply allow every part of your body to relax. Once you have done this, mentally check your body for any remaining areas of tension, and allow them to relax. Most people find the tension in their necks and shoulders to be the hardest to release.

Once you feel that your body is completely relaxed, focus your attention on your nostrils. Feel the breath coming in and going out. Concentrate on your breathing. Naturally, odd thoughts will pop into your mind from time to time. This is perfectly normal, and there is no need to worry when this occurs. All you need to do is let them go as soon as you become consciously aware of them and then focus on your breathing once more. Ultimately, there will be no thoughts. Once this point is reached, you are ready to recite your mantra.

As was mentioned earlier, it takes time and practice to become proficient at meditation. It is essential that you master this phase of writing your own magic. The ability to meditate is of supreme importance. It allows you to reach your Higher Self, the god within you. Whatever it is that you desire can then be implanted in the deepest part of your mind. Whatever is placed there will ultimately manifest itself in your life. Take whatever time is necessary to master this skill. Do not become concerned if your mind keeps wandering while you are meditating.

Everyone experiences this. It can be extremely difficult to quieten our minds and temporarily forget about the worries and pressures of daily life. However, regular daily practice will ensure ultimate success. I find it best to meditate at the same time every day whenever possible.

If you find it extremely hard to relax, you may need to record a progressive relaxation tape for yourself. A suggested script can be found in Appendix A. However, do not become reliant on your tape. Ultimately, you want to become able to do this exercise anywhere at any time. Your options are much more limited if you need to have a cassette recorder and tape with you. Once you become proficient at relaxing with the tape, see if you can relax just as easily without it. In practice, I occasionally use a recorded tape simply for variation.

Other Methods of Meditation

There are many ways in which you can achieve the right meditative state in which to send your desires out into the universe.

Color Meditation

Sit in a comfortable position with your eyes closed. Take three deep breaths and say to yourself, "Relax, relax deeply," each time you exhale. Remain aware of your breathing and feel the relaxation in your body.

Next, imagine yourself surrounded by a cloud of energy that is the most beautiful red you have ever seen. Allow yourself to become completely immersed in the red color, and let it permeate every cell of your body.

Gradually allow the red to slowly fade and be replaced by orange, again the most vibrant orange color you have ever seen. Allow this orange to reach every part of your body, so that you are completely enfolded by it, both inside and out. Once you reach this state, allow the orange to fade and replace it with yellow. Allow this to reach every fiber of your being, and then replace it with green, followed by blue, indigo, and finally violet.

Once you have experienced the sensations of each color of the rainbow, allow the violet to disappear, and imagine yourself bathed in a pure white light.

Golden Light Meditation

Make yourself comfortable, close your eyes, and take three deep breaths. Feel the pleasant relaxation in your body.

Now visualize a beautiful ball of golden light a few inches above your head. Visualize this light slowly coming down and entering the top of your head. Feel the golden light relaxing every part of your body that it reaches. Feel it slowly moving down your body, relaxing every cell it meets on the way.

Finally, allow the ball of golden light to bathe your feet in its wonderful, soothing, restful glow. Allow it to remain there for about a minute, and then allow it to rise up through your body again, until it is back in position just above your head.

If desired, you can do this exercise two or three times, becoming more and more relaxed every time.

Concentration Meditation

This method of meditation involves looking at something specific, while at the same time deliberately relaxing your mind and body. I usually use a mandala or pictorial yantra for this.[2] A pictorial yantra has a central point, known as a *bindu,* which acts as the focal point for meditation. In fact, a simple dot can be regarded as a yantra, and used for meditation purposes. (See chapter 10 for more information on mandalas and yantras.) A crystal ball is also commonly used as a focal point for meditation. You can focus your attention on virtually anything. Let us assume that you are using an attractive floral display.

Sit down comfortably several feet away from the flowers and look at them. Take three deep breaths, exhaling slowly, and then forget about your breathing. Simply look at the flowers. Notice the different colors and textures of the flowers. Look at the different greens of the various stalks.

After a while, you will notice that the display tends to merge into a homogenous mixture. You will cease to notice the individual colors or separate flowers, and will instead be drawn deeper into a quiet, meditative, contemplative state.

Counting Backward Meditation

Relax comfortably with your eyes closed. Picture a large blank movie screen in your mind. Imagine that the number one hundred is written on this screen in huge numbers. Look at this number and then allow it to dissolve until it has completely disappeared from your mind. Imagine the number ninety-nine written on the screen. Again make this number dissolve and disappear. Continue to count down from one hundred until you feel that you are relaxed enough in both body and mind to start reciting the mantra. Most of the time, I find I am completely relaxed by the time I reach ninety, though there have been occasions when I've reached fifty before proceeding to the next stage.

Walking Meditation

Although it may sound surprising, it is perfectly possible to meditate while walking. In fact, you have probably done it many times in the past without knowing it. If you have ever walked anywhere while your mind was preoccupied, you have performed a walking meditation.

I find it easiest to do a walking meditation while silently repeating a mantra to myself (see the following section for examples). The mantra should repeated in time with your footsteps, and is a highly effective and rapid way of achieving a totally relaxed state.

Mantra Recitation

Mantra meditation is arguably the best-known form of meditation. A mantra is a short phrase or sentence that is repeated, usually out loud, over and over again. Jan Gonda claims that mantras are an effective means of "coming into touch or identifying oneself with the essence of the divinity which is present in the mantra."[3]

The most famous mantra is *Om mani padme hum*, which is usually translated as "O, thou jewel of the lotus." Although this a correct translation, it is a rather superficial one. This remarkable mantra signifies much more than that. *Mani* can represent anything precious, including an enlightened mind. *Padme* represents the lotus blossom, as well as spiritual endfoldment, or awakening. As *Om* represents the universal body, in this mantra we have body, mind, and spirit. In Singapore this mantra is considered to mean "May there be peace in the world."

Om is pronounced "aum." This word has special significance, as when it is spoken it begins from the deepest part of the throat and ends with the lips closed. This relates to alpha and omega, the beginning and the end. The word *Om* depicts the universal cosmic consciousness. *Mani padme* is pronounced "mah-nee pahd-may," and *hum* is pronounced "haum," as it is a variation of *Om.*

To say the mantra, take a long deep breath. Half the exhalation is used to say "Om," followed by "mani padme," and a lengthy "hum" at the end.

You will feel a powerful vibration, almost like a hum, as you say this mantra. As you repeat it over and over again you will gradually feel more and more in tune with the infinite. This is the purpose of using mantras. They open up doorways to invisible worlds, and provide access to the universal life force. Mantras also help you to gain peace of mind and contentment.

Om mani padme hum is the best overall mantra to use, and can be used on all occasions. You need not use this mantra, although I recommend that you do, especially at the start. You can create your own mantra using any phrase that appeals to you. Some mantras consist of groups of syllables that have no particular meaning. It is the rhythm and pitch of the chant that make them work. Yet, mantras almost always have specific purposes. Other mantras that can be used on specific occasions include the following:

> ***Om aeeng kaleeng soo.*** This mantra is used if your request relates to a greater proficiency with words, both written and spoken.
>
> ***Om shareeng hareeng kaleeng.*** This mantra is used if your request relates to wealth.

Om aeeng hareeng kaleeng. This mantra is used if your request relates to freedom from worry and greater happiness.

Om shareeng hareeng kaleeng. This mantra is used if your request relates to sexual relationships. However, it should be used with care, as it also relates to conception.

Om hareeng. This mantra is used if your request relates to your health, particularly recovering from an illness.

Om aeeng kaleeng hareeng. This mantra is used for protective purposes and helps you achieve your desires.

You will notice that these mantras are similar to each other. The individual words are called *Samput,* and their positioning in the mantra affects both its intent and the outcome.

You should repeat the mantra you are using for five minutes. Mantras are extremely useful as a form of meditative device. At the end of five minutes you will be in the perfect position to ask for your request to be granted.

Sending Out Your Request

The method that I was taught years ago to do this is simple and effective. All you need to do is set fire to the piece of paper on which your desire is written.

As it burns, imagine your desire going out into the universe.

Fire has been used in magical rites for thousands of years. It has always been considered holy, and ancient peoples believed it to be a gift from the gods. Fire worship was common in ancient primitive cultures where it was believed either to be a god itself or a symbol of divine power. This worship was a mixture of praise and fear. It is not surprising that myths from nearly every culture contain stories of how humans came to possess fire.

Fire can both heat and burn. Life exists purely because of the fire from the sun, but a raging fire can destroy life. Consequently, it needs to be treated carefully. A traditional image of domestic bliss is a family seated around the hearth—safe, comfortable, and protected.

Fire was one of the four elements of the ancients in the West, and is still a vital element in magical practices today. In the East there are the five elements of wood, fire, earth, metal, and water. During the Chinese New Year people carry and display beautiful lanterns to represent the fire element, and fireworks are set off.

In the Christian tradition, fire is an incarnation of the Holy Spirit. In Jeremiah 23:29 we read: "Is not my word like as a fire, saith the Lord." God appears by fire on several occasions, most notably when he appears to Moses in a burning bush (Exodus 3:2).[4]

This is an example of the spiritual fire that burns, but does not consume. In Buddhism, one symbol of Buddha is a pillar of fire.

In alchemy, fire was depicted as a triangle and was always the unifying element. Fire is also frequently used to symbolize union with the godhead, another reason why it is a popular choice for magical purposes. Fire is also used as a metaphor for desire. Although this symbolism is usually sexual, it encompasses all forms of desire. These all suit our purposes perfectly.

Once your request has completely burned, give thanks to the universe for all the blessings in your life. I prefer to spend a few minutes enjoying the pleasant feelings of relaxation before returning to full normal consciousness. I allow myself to think about my request, before becoming aware of my breathing. I gradually become aware of my surroundings and any outside noises I may hear. Finally, I open my eyes and stretch.

Many people like to end their rituals in a formal manner. How you do this is entirely up to you. You may like to make a formal bow to each of the four cardinal directions. If you have used candles, blow them out immediately after bowing in their direction.

Members of the Order of the Golden Dawn finish their meditations with the Sign of Silence. To do this, stand with your feet together and hands by your sides. Stamp once with your left foot. Touch the center of your lower lip with the forefinger of your left hand with the other fingers and thumb closed.

There is no need to spend any more time thinking about your request. It has gone out into the universe and all you need to do is remain confident that it will be granted. Some people find it almost anticlimactic to end on this note. After the build-up of setting the scene and completing the ritual, they expect something exciting and dramatic at the end. I must admit I look forward to the quietness and peace at the end of the ceremony. Hopefully, you will feel the same. If you inwardly expect shooting stars and an angel chorus, you should do what a student of mine does. She hugs herself and shouts, "It's mine! It's mine! It's mine!"

Of course, it is not always easy to bring your attention back to your everyday life. You may find that a brisk walk, or some other form of exercise, is required to return you to the mundane world.

Some people feel frustrated that there is nothing more they can do. In fact there is, and that will be covered in the next chapter.

Paper Burning in the East

In the East, paper burning is a fact of life and is performed all over Asia, even in places where the practice is officially discouraged or forbidden.[5]

The Chinese New Year is a time for feasting, enjoyment, and family visits. Homes are thoroughly cleaned and decorated with paper images. A poster of the

Hearth or Kitchen God, which has been displayed for a whole year, will be replaced with a new one. It is believed that on the twenty-third day of the twelfth month this god reports on what the family has done during the previous year. Consequently, his lips are frequently smeared with sticky honey to ensure that he either cannot open his mouth or has only sweet things to report.[6] New images of the other gods, particularly one of the many Gods of Wealth, will also be displayed on the second day of the New Year.

On the fifteenth day of the first month is the Lantern Festival, during which sacrifices are made to the hundred gods in heaven.[7] Huge mounds of paper money, prayer sheets, and paper horses are burned. The horses and money are to make sure that the prayers reach their destination. The prayer sheets are fine examples of people writing their own magic.

The next occasion when paper objects are burned is the Qingming Festival, during the second or third month of the lunar year. Graves of ancestors are thoroughly cleaned and sacrifices of food and a huge variety of paper objects are made for the ancestors' happiness and comfort on the other side.[8] In the past, the offering consisted of paper money and paper clothes, but nowadays it is just as likely to include paper items such as television sets, cards, houses, beer cans, and DVDs.

During the Feast of Hungry Ghosts, held in the seventh month of the lunar year, many of the same items are burned. However, in addition to sending objects to their ancestors, people also burn items to placate any wandering spirits.

The seventh day of the seventh moon, known as the Feast of the Double Seventh, is the most important day of the year for unmarried women. According to legend, this is the day when magpies form a bridge across the Milky Way to enable the Weaving Maiden to visit her lover, the Cowherd. Because of this, unmarried women consider the Weaving Maiden their patroness. The Weaving Maiden is sent many paper offerings, and fortunetellers are kept busy on this important day in the lunar calendar. The paper offerings include combs, mirrors, clothes, and written messages.

On the ninth day of the ninth month, Chongyang, the Mounting the Heights Festival, is celebrated. In Penang, Malaysia, many people make a pilgrimage to the Temple of the Nine Venerable Sovereigns on this day, and wear paper amulets.

There are many other times during the year when paper objects are burned. Many different gods receive offerings on their days of birth, and the gods who look after different occupations are also rewarded in the same way. For instance, Wen Ti, the God of Literature, is worshipped on the third moon and again during the eighth moon by people who make their living as writers. He is usually depicted holding a pen and a book containing four characters that read "Heaven decides literary success."[9] Paper money and requests are sent to him on the days he is worshipped in the hope that heaven will help the literary efforts of the people making the offerings.

When someone dies, the family will light candles, offer food, and burn ceremonial papers to make the deceased's path to the other world as smooth as possible. The coffin will be accompanied to the burial ground by a wide variety of paper offerings such as checkbooks, credit cards, houses, cars, and television sets, which are burned by the graveside. Paper money is frequently tossed into the air on the way to the graveyard also.

The habit of burning paper offerings has survived intact to the present day. In some parts of Asia, restrictions are placed on how and when paper offerings can be made, but it seems certain that the joss shops who sell spirit papers are in no danger of dying out.

Candle Burning

Another method of sending your request out into the universe is by burning a candle that has your request inscribed on the sides. Naturally, your request has to be written in as few words as possible.

If you have the time, you might wish to make your own candles. I know several people who do this. They enjoy thinking about their request as they make the candles, and believe that this adds power and energy to their requests. I have made my own candles in the past, but nowadays I use commercially made candles. This is purely a matter of time. If I had more spare time, I would probably start making my own candles again.

I prefer to use a square-shaped candle as it is easier to carve the words into this than into a round or irregular-shaped candle. Many people believe that triangular-shaped candles amplify your request as it goes out into the universe and are therefore more effective. Yet, a square-shaped candle is more solid and grounded. If your request relates to financial matters or anything to do with the home and family, a square-shaped candle is likely to be the most effective. If your request relates to communication or creativity, experiment with triangular and cylinder-shaped candles. There is particular power in writing your request in a spiral around a circular candle.

You can write your request in English, or you may prefer to use a secret alphabet such as Theban or Templar.[10] Three secret alphabets are included in Appendix C. When using a magical alphabet you have to concentrate more than you do when you write the words in English. This adds extra power to the ritual. It can also be used to keep your message a secret from others.

The color of the candle is important. A white candle is satisfactory for all requests, but you may prefer to use a different color for a specific task. In the East, red means good luck and gold means money. That is why the decor of most Chinese restaurants includes red and gold in its color scheme. Consequently, if you are wanting good fortune to enter your life, you might choose a red candle. If your request involves money, you might decide to choose a gold candle.

If your request relates to your purpose in life, you should use a candle that relates to your numerological Life Path.[11] Your Life Path is determined by making a sum of your month, day, and year of birth, and reducing it to a single digit. There are two exceptions to this. If in the course of reducing down to a single digit you come across the number 11 or 22 you stop there and do not reduce them down to 2 or 4.

Here is an example. Suppose you were born on July 12, 1973. The mathematics look like this:

> 7 month
> 12 day
> <u>1973</u> year
> 1992, and 1 + 9 + 9 + 2 = 21, and 2 + 1 = 3

This person has a Life Path number of 3.

Here is another example. A friend of mine has her birthday on February 29, 1944:

> 2 month
> 29 day
> <u>1944</u> year
> 1975, and 1 + 9 + 7 + 5 = 22

She has a Life Path number of 22 as the numbers 11 and 22 are not reduced further.

We create a vertical sum of the numbers because 11s and 22s can be lost if we add them in a straight line. This is the case with my friend's date of birth:

> 2 (month) + 2 + 9 (day)
> + 1 + 9 + 4 + 4 (year) = 31, and 3 + 1 = 4

Each number Life Path relates to a specific color:

    1—red
    2—orange
    3—yellow
    4—green
    5—blue
    6—indigo (dark blue)
    7—violet
    8—pink
    9—bronze
    11—silver
    22—gold

Use a candle that relates to your Life Path color if your request relates to the direction of your life.

You may find when you are choosing a candle that a certain candle almost leaps into your hand, as if it has chosen you, rather than the other way around. Do not hesitate. Choose this candle whenever this occurs. Many times I have made up my mind to buy a certain colored candle, but left the store with a totally different color. All the colors have meanings, and for general requests it is a good idea to choose a color that relates to your request, except, of course, when a candle chooses you.

Meanings of the Colors

White

White relates to purity, innocence, and truth. It is excellent for new starts and whenever energy is required. It removes negativity and promotes a positive outlook to all aspects of your life. It is an excellent color for any purpose.

Red

Red creates enthusiasm and energy. Its color relates to health, strength, passion, blood, and our most primal instincts. Red candles should be burned if your request relates to love, sex, energy, or health. It is also a good color for all ambitious requests.

Orange

Orange relates to all close relationships. If you are having difficulty in getting on with anyone and your request relates to this, orange is the perfect color to choose.

Yellow

Yellow relates to the intellect, creativity, and expressing the joys of life. If you are hoping to enhance your creativity or gain more enjoyment from life, yellow is a good color to use.

Green

Green has always been considered a healing and nurturing color. It relates to emotional balance, peace of mind, and steady progress toward your goals. It also relates to hope, confidence, and procreation. It is also the color that relates to money, abundance, success, and luck. If your request relates to any of these things, a green candle is the right one to choose.

Blue

Blue relates to versatility, travel, and instant money. It represents truth, inspiration, health, wisdom, loyalty, and peace of mind. It is a good color for people who are self-employed. Blue also provides enthusiasm, an abundance of ideas, and hope for the future. It is a good color for people who are in love. Choose a blue candle if your request relates to any of these. Blue is also a color of protection, and any blue objects in your home help protect you from any negativity that might come your way. A blue candle is a good choice if you are experiencing negativity in any area of your life.

Indigo (Dark Blue)

It is rare to find a true indigo-colored candle, but dark blue ones make a good substitute. This color relates to home, family, security, and care and responsibility for others. It is a nurturing color, and should be chosen if your request relates to helping others—particularly family members—in any way.

Violet and Purple

These have always been considered spiritual colors and should be used if your request relates to spiritual or philosophical growth. They also relate to intelligence and knowledge, and make a good choice if your request relates to study, learning, or psychic development. Violet is also a restful color and makes a good tonic for people who are overtired or suffering from stress.

Pink

Pink has always been considered a romantic color, so a candle of this color should be used if your request relates to love in any way. However, pink also relates to long-term financial success, and can also be used if your request relates to business dealings. Pink is a pure, honest, upright color that relates well to noble intentions. It also represents gentleness, affection, loyalty, and honor.

Bronze and Autumn Tones

Bronze relates to humanitarian undertakings, and should be used if your request concerns helping others. It is more universal than indigo, which relates to helping people close to you. If your request involves helping others on a large scale, this is the candle to choose.

Silver

Silver relates to inner growth and development. If your request relates to intuition or the occult, this is a good color to choose. This color also relates well to requests concerning the arts and anything beautiful.

Gold

Gold is the perfect color to choose if your request relates to something large-scale and important. If you are hoping to head in new directions and take on fresh and different challenges, this is the color to choose.

Brown

Brown is a color that is rooted firmly in the ground. Consequently, it is a good color to choose if your request relates to property and real estate. Brown is also related to sorrow. If your request relates to righting a wrong that you have committed, a brown candle is the best one to choose.

Black

Black is considered a negative color, and I have noticed that many people are suspicious, and even scared, of black candles. You should not use black candles if you consider them evil or dangerous. However, black candles are extremely powerful and can be used if your request involves uncovering secrets and determining the truth.

If you have problems in deciding which color is right for you, choose white. White candles can be used for any purpose. Consequently, I always keep a small supply of them ready for whenever I need them.

I like to inscribe my message onto the candle with a heated knitting needle. A friend of mine prefers to use a penknife and is capable of doing extremely neat work with it. Wiccans often carve the words with a white-handled knife. They frequently write their request in Theban, rather than English.[12] Some types of marking pens allow you to simply write your request on the sides of the candle. Experiment and use whatever method seems most appropriate for you.

I prefer to inscribe my message late at night when there is little chance of being disturbed. Writing a message on a candle takes time and concentration, and I believe that this helps make the process more effective.

After writing my message, I wrap the candle in a cloth and put it away until the next day. It does not matter what type of material you wrap your candle in, as long as the cloth is aesthetically pleasing to you.

Dressing the Candle

When you are ready to send your message out into the universe, wipe the candle carefully with good-quality olive oil. There are commercial oils available for dressing candles in this way, but olive oil works extremely well and is also easy to obtain. Use a fine cloth and always wipe the oil onto the candle from the center out to the two ends. Start at the middle of the candle and work your way up to the top. Then, again starting from the middle, rub the candle down to the bottom.

Think about your purpose in using the candle while you are dressing it. This can almost become a ritual in itself, and is an essential part of the process. If you use the same candle a number of times, you must dress, or anoint, it each time before use.

The purpose of this part of the process is to remove any negativity from the candle. This may have been caused while the candle was being made, or absorbed while the candle was waiting for you to buy it.

Blessing the Candle

Once the candle has been cleansed, it should be blessed. Place the candle on your right palm and then rest this palm on your left palm. This creates a circle of energy. Close your eyes and think of your purpose in burning the candle. Visualize yourself as you will be once the request has come into fruition. Bless the candle for its part in the process. Finally, thank the architect of the universe for enabling your dreams to become manifest. Take a deep breath and say "Thank you" three times as you exhale. It makes no difference if you say these words silently or out loud.

Burning the Candle

Now it is time to burn the candle. It is best to do this in the evening when it is dark outside. Place the candle on your home altar if you have one. Otherwise clear a table and place it in the center. I have a large blue cloth that I cover the table with before starting.

Light the candle and then turn off the lights in the room. Sit in a position where you can look directly at the flame. As the smoke drifts upward, think about your request and how the smoke is taking it out into the universe.

Stay watching the smoke for as long as feels comfortable. I find about a half hour is the right length of time for me. Do not blow the candle out. Either cover the wick or use your fingers to dowse the flame.

Of course, your request is not completely transmitted until the entire candle has been consumed, so you will need to do this ritual several times until the candle has completely burned down. However, word of your request will have gone out into the universe from the moment you lit the candle the first time. Consequently, you should regard each additional session as reinforcement to the original one. I find the repetition comforting and reassuring. I prefer to burn a candle over a period of successive days. If I feel overly tired or stressed on one evening, I will postpone the burning until a time when I felt relaxed and in control. If possible, burn your candle over a series of evenings, but do not worry if you do not perform this magic on every consecutive night.

Dissolving Ink

When I was twenty-one I spent a year in Glasgow, Scotland. My landlady was an eccentric old lady who had never married. Everywhere she went, even from room to room in her home, she carried a broom. I discovered after a few months that the broom was for protection, as she did not feel comfortable with men and lived in fear that one day some man would attack her. This surprised me, as all of her boarders were men. If I had been her, I would have had women boarders. She was in her late seventies when I knew her, and had never been attacked, so maybe the presence of a broom worked after all. She was small, but forbidding, and it took me quite a few months before I felt completely relaxed with her. In fact, it was our mutual interest in divination that enabled us to become friends.

She had an interesting method of writing magic that she had learned from her grandmother. She used a small white plate of bone china. It was about five inches in diameter. On this plate she would write her request using a fountain pen and blue ink that dissolved in water. She had beautiful copper-plate handwriting and was able to write lengthy requests in a tiny script.

Once she had written down her request, she would hold the plate in front of her, and gaze into it while taking deep breaths. Each exhalation sounded like a sigh.

After several deep breaths she would put the plate down and close her eyes for about half an hour. During this time she thought about her request and why she wanted it. At the end of this time, she would get up and wash the plate in a bowl of boiled water from her kettle. The ink was normally still quite wet at this time and dissolved quickly in the boiling water. My landlady would dry her special plate and put it away carefully before drinking the water she had washed it in.

I used this technique for some years after learning it from my landlady and found it worked extremely well. I quickly discovered why she used bone china. Fountain pens appear to write much better on good quality china than on cheaper ware. If I still owned a fountain pen I would probably still be using this method. If you wish to try this method and do not own a fountain pen, try using a felt-tipped marker with ink that dissolves in water.

The only other method I have seen involved invisible ink. Many years ago I met an elderly man on top of a sacred mountain. He had several paper darts with him. I noticed that he sent them off into flight from the four cardinal directions, and asked him what he was doing. He had written his requests on the paper in invisible ink before turning them into darts. He recited a brief spell as he launched each dart. He was a pleasant man, but seemed embarrassed to be seen launching darts into space. He disappeared before I could ask him any further questions.

Taoist Temple Wish

This method uses a number of elements that we have discussed earlier. I first saw this in a Taoist temple, but have since seen it practiced in people's homes as well. In its most simple form it involves a blessing that is written down on three strips of paper by the temple medium. The person who has petitioned for the wish or blessing kneels down in front of an altar where one of the medium's secretaries burns the first strip of paper and pours the ashes into a glass of water. The petitioner drinks the liquid, and, in effect, drinks in the wish or blessing. The second strip is then set on fire and, while it is burning, is passed over the petitioner's body and head to provide a shield of protection. The third strip of paper is placed into a green envelope and given to the petitioner to keep on his or her person.

There is no reason why you cannot perform this entire ceremony on your own. Write down your request or blessing on three slips of paper. Burn and drink the first one in a glass of water. Set fire to the second one and turn around while it is burning to provide you with a circle of protection. Place the third one into an envelope, preferably green, and carry this around with you. Every time you see the envelope, or read the slip inside, you will be reminded of your request. Keep the envelope until the request has been fulfilled, and then burn it. Make a ceremony of this. Thank the universe for granting your request as you set fire to the envelope. Watch the smoke drift upward as you give thanks for all the blessings in your life.

In the final analysis, it does not matter which method you use to send your request out into the universe. They all work. You might want to experiment with all of them and see which method you prefer. You may also decide to use varying methods at different times. The important thing is that you are happy with the ritual and feel confident that your request has been sent.

Magnetizing Yourself

Chapter 8

Words are also actions, and actions are a kind of words.

RALPH WALDO EMERSON (1803–1882)

IT MAY SEEM STRANGE that you write down your request, create a ritual to send it out into the universe, and then simply stop. In a sense, you don't stop, of course. You need to maintain a sense of positive expectancy that your request will be granted. You should have no doubt whatsoever that whatever it is you asked for will occur. After all, at the very deepest level, your will is also the Creator's will. Therefore, the architect of the universe will grant your request.

There is an interesting concept known as "luck." Some people seem to receive good luck all the time, while other people receive nothing but bad luck. No matter how unlucky you may have been in the past, the techniques in this book will enable you to become one of the lucky ones in future. In fact, I do not believe in luck, I believe that we create our own destiny by the way we think. If you consider yourself unlucky, that is what you will receive until you change your thoughts. Lucky people have a positive expectancy. They expect good things to happen to them, and they invariably do.

It is natural to feel despondent when things don't work out the way we want them to. However, even in these situations naturally lucky people think, "It didn't work this time, but next time it will." These people quickly get over their depression and start planning ahead again. They expect good things to happen to them, and of course, that is exactly what they receive.

It is vital that you remain positive while you are waiting for your requests to be granted. By doing this you put luck on your side.

There is no knowing how long it will take for your desires to become realized. Usually, simple requests are manifested quickly, while more complex desires take longer. However, this is not always the case.

Some years ago, I needed several thousand dollars to attend a convention in another country. I was eager to attend as one of the speakers had a wealth of information on a topic of mutual interest. Since I needed a large sum of money, I did not expect a quick result. However, within hours of sending out my request, someone called and asked me to do some work for them. The fee offered was sufficient to cover all the costs of attending the convention.

You need to maintain a sense of positive expectancy until your goal is realized. Naturally, you will experience doubt and uncertainty at times. Whenever you catch yourself thinking negatively, remind yourself that the matter is now in the hands of the universe and it will happen. These feelings will be few and far between once you magnetize yourself.

A magnet both attracts and repels. Naturally, you will want to repel any negative energy that prevents you from achieving your goals. Likewise, you will want to attract your goals to you.

It is important to magnetize yourself so strongly that any thoughts of failure vanish before they are fully formed. Your mind must remain calm, serene, and supremely confident that your desire will be granted. There are many ways of doing this.

Thoughts, Feelings, and Emotions

While you are waiting for your request to become a reality, spend time thinking about how your life will be different once it is achieved. In your mind's eye see as clearly as possible the beneficial changes that will take place. Picture yourself enjoying the pleasures and advantages of your new life once your goal has been achieved. You can think about your request whenever you have a few spare moments.

Become aware of your feelings and emotions concerning your request. Naturally, you will have considerable emotional attachment to a positive outcome. Allow these feelings and emotions full play when thinking about your goals. Desires that have an emotional component to them are always more successful than requests that have been worked out clinically and logically.

Affirmations

Another method is to use affirmations as frequently as possible. Affirmations are positive suggestions that are deliberately implanted into the subconscious mind. Affirmations also remind us that we need to keep aware of our thoughts, and that we alone are responsible for our actions. We all have some fifty to sixty thousand thoughts a day. Many of these are negative thoughts. As we become what we think about, it is important to think more positive thoughts than negative ones. Whenever you find yourself thinking a negative thought, switch it around and make it positive, or say an affirmation to yourself. It can be helpful to remember that our thoughts create our reality. We need to make sure that we are thinking as many positive thoughts as possible.

You can say affirmations to yourself at any time. They are more effective when said out loud, as this enables you to hear them as you say them. You can repeat them in different ways, for example, by placing the emphasis on different words each time. You can sing them, too, if you wish.

However, affirmations can also be used silently. I always say my affirmations silently while waiting in line at the bank. Naturally, I do not say them out loud in this situation.

Affirmations should be phrased in the present tense, as if you already have the quality you desire. Here are some general affirmations that you can use. It is a good idea to write out your own affirmations that relate specifically to you and your desires. You should carry these around with you so you can read them in spare moments:

"I am in tune with the universe."

"I attract nothing but good into my life."

"I am a loving and caring person."

"I am successful."

These are general, all-purpose affirmations that can be extremely helpful. However, you should also compose specific affirmations that relate to you and your specific desires. You might, for instance, say, "It is early September, and I am sitting in the living room of my new home overlooking the Pacific Ocean." As you say this, you will naturally picture yourself luxuriating in the comfort of your surroundings and enjoying the magnificent view. Your subconscious mind cannot tell the difference between this imaginary picture and the reality, and will work to make it become part of your life.

Amulets and Talismans

An *amulet* is an object that is worn or carried to protect a person from harm and to bring good luck. They are usually made from stone or metal, and are frequently engraved. However, they can be made from almost anything. For instance, a four-leaf clover and a lucky rabbit's foot are both examples of amulets.

A *talisman* is an object that is believed to possess magical properties. Talismans are frequently made from parchment, papyrus, pottery, or shell, but like amulets, can also be made from stone or metal. They are intended to bring about a specific result from an event that has not yet occurred.

The words amulet and talisman are frequently used as synonyms. This is not correct. Amulets are used for more general purposes than talismans. They provide protection and attract good luck. Talismans are used for more specific applications, and can be made for both good and evil purposes. In this book we will be discussing only the positive uses of talismans.

In antiquity, there were a number of natural talismans which were objects that simply had to be obtained to become effective. They were:

Mandragora, which inspired love.

Topaz, which drove away negative thoughts.

Ruby, which calmed people who were over-excited.

Hyena skin, which made people invulnerable.

Bezoar, which cured virtually everything.[1]

I first became interested in amulets and talismans while in Thailand more than twenty years ago. Virtually everyone there seemed to use one. Most people wore an amulet of some sort, but some people never went anywhere without a huge collection of them hanging around their necks on a gold chain. Thai people did not hesitate to spend large sums of money on an amulet that they believed would ward off evil or attract good luck.

Amulets and talismans are included here because the power that they possess depends largely on the writing that is inscribed upon them, or placed within them, whether that writing is understood or not. Consequently, it is not uncommon for the inscription to be written in a language that is not known to the owner of the amulet or talisman.

Amulets and talismans could be described as good luck charms. People have carried such charms on them for thousands of years, both to create good luck and to avert bad luck. Although some people in the West think that carrying an amulet or talisman is simply a primitive superstition, it is worth noting that Americans spend more than $130 million a year on good luck charms.[2]

Talismans are frequently used for protection, of which the St. Christopher medal is a good example. Since St. Christopher is the patron saint of travellers, many people have these attached to their cars. Interestingly, when the U.S. Navy failed to put their Vanguard rockets into orbit in 1968, the contractors said that this was because the rockets did not contain St. Christopher medals. A medal was attached to the next rocket, and it went into orbit with no problems whatsoever.[3]

A well-known Jewish talisman is the *mezuzah,* which is a roll of parchment containing the statutes from the Book of Deuteronomy. It is carried in a small case or affixed to the lintel of doorways because the Bible says: "And thou shalt write them upon the posts of thy house, and on thy gates."[4] The mezuzah is just one example of the enormous variety of permitted and forbidden amulets that the Jewish people can choose from. And they are not alone. For thousands of years, people all around the world have had their own amulets and talismans to ensure protection and good luck.

Amulets and talismans can be made out of virtually anything. They can be something as simple as a pebble found on the seashore, or a sheet of paper containing words of protection. Of course, they can also be ornate and valuable, such as a necklace or ring. Traditionally, they were usually made of precious stones or valuable metal, and were worn to provide protection and to ward off disease and the "evil eye." Rings made of precious stones and metal became popular talismans.

King Solomon wore a talismanic ring, in the stone of which he was able to clairvoyantly see everything he needed to know. A ring was an important part of Hebrew attire because it contained a person's signet, or seal. Women also wore rings as jewelry.[5]

There is an interesting story about a ring that Queen Elizabeth I gave to the Earl of Essex to use as a talisman. Queen Elizabeth was extremely superstitious, which is one reason why she always wore so much jewelry. Her clothes and even her coach were covered with valuable rubies, emeralds, and diamonds.

At the time she gave Lord Essex the ring, he was one of her favorites, and she presented it to him as a token of her affection. She also told him that if he ever fell out of favor with her, all he had to do was send her the ring and the mere sight of it would provide instant forgiveness.

When the Earl of Essex was imprisoned in the Tower of London awaiting execution, he remembered what the queen had said. Unfortunately, he felt unable to trust any of his attendants. One day, looking out from his cell, he saw a small boy walking past and called him over. Lord Essex bribed the boy to take the ring to Lady Scrope, the earl's cousin, and ask her to send it to the queen. The boy mistakenly took the ring to the Countess of Nottingham instead, who was Lady Scrope's sister. The countess showed the ring to her husband, who loathed Lord Essex. He insisted that the ring and the message remain hidden.

Meanwhile, the queen was waiting, fully expecting the ring to arrive. In fact, she had even repealed the warrant of execution. When the ring did not appear, she assumed that Lord Essex was too proud to appeal to her and the execution went ahead.[6]

In his book *The Magus*, Francis Barrett describes how talismanic rings should be made: "When any star ascends in the horoscope (fortunately), with a fortunate aspect or conjunction of the moon, we proceed to take a stone and herb, that is under that star, and likewise make a ring of the metal that is corresponding to the star; and in the ring, under the stone, put the herb or root, not forgetting to inscribe the effect, image, name, and character, as also the proper suffume (a decoction of root, herb, flowers, seed, etc.)."[7]

Fortunately, it is not necessary to go to these lengths to make a talismanic ring for yourself. All you need to do is find an attractive ring that contains a stone that relates to your zodiac sign or month of birth.

Belief that there is a special stone for each month of the year goes back at least two thousand years when Josephus made a connection between the twelve stones of the high priest's breastplate and the months of the year.[8] However, it was not until the eighteenth century when the wearing of specific natal stones became popular in Poland.[9] At that time it was felt that people should own twelve stones, one for each month of the year, and wear the correct stone each month for therapeutic and talismanic reasons.

The specific stones for each month have changed slightly over the centuries. Here are the most commonly accepted stones:

> January—garnet
> February—amethyst
> March—aquamarine, bloodstone
> April—diamond, sapphire
> May—emerald
> June—pearl, moonstone, cat's-eye, turquoise,
> agate

July — ruby, turquoise, onyx
August — peridot, sardonyx, carnelian,
  moonstone, topaz
September — sapphire, chrysolite
October — opal, beryl, tourmaline
November — topaz
December — turquoise, ruby, bloodstone,
  lapis lazuli

You may prefer to use the stone that relates to your astrological sign:

Aries — diamond, ruby, red jasper
Taurus — lapis lazuli, sapphire
Gemini — citrine, yellow agate
Cancer — pearl, moonstone
Leo — tiger's-eye, dendritic agate
Virgo — green jasper, sardonyx
Libra — sapphire, aquamarine
Scorpio — ruby, opal, red jasper
Sagittarius — topaz
Capricorn — turquoise, smoky quartz
Aquarius — amethyst
Pisces — moonstone, rose quartz

You can also choose a stone that relates to the day of the week you were born on:

Sunday — topaz, diamond
Monday — pearl, crystal
Tuesday — ruby, emerald

Wednesday—amethyst, loadstone
Thursday—sapphire, carnelian
Friday—emerald, cat's-eye
Saturday—turquoise, diamond

There is even a talismanic gem that relates to each day of the week:

Sunday—pearl
Monday—emerald
Tuesday—topaz
Wednesday—turquoise
Thursday—sapphire
Friday—ruby
Saturday—amethyst

Finally, as the talisman is going to be something that you will want to wear or keep close to you, it is important that it is something that appeals to you aesthetically. If the stones for your month, zodiac sign, or day of the week do not appeal to you, choose a stone that resonates with you.

To do this, look at a variety of different stones. Often a particular stone will have a special aura about it that sets it apart from the other stones. Naturally, this is the one you should buy. You can also find the right stone by using psychometry. Hold the stones that appeal to you in the palm of your hand one at a time. You will experience a response from one or more of the stones. Your hand might feel warm, or cool, or you may simply have a sense that the stone you are holding is right for you. Buy the one that responds best to you, and use it as your personal talisman.

At one time it was thought that you should not buy a precious stone for yourself. Those days have long gone. After all, you have worked for your money in the first place. You expend your time and energy in exchange for your money. Now you are simply exchanging some of that money to purchase something that will protect and help you.

Talismans are important in a number of ways. First, every time you notice your talisman it will remind you of your desire. Second, talismans provide protection for the person wearing or carrying them. And third, talismans can be charged with positive energy to help attract to you whatever it is you desire. I find it extremely helpful to carry around a personal talisman that relates specifically to my desire.

Making Your Own Talisman

It is generally easier to find a suitable amulet or talisman than it is to make one. However, if you have knowledge and expertise, there is no reason why you cannot make one for yourself.

Amulets are usually intended to be attractive to look at. As a result, you need artistic skills to make them. Talismans are much easier to make. The easiest ones consist of words on paper. There are a number of ways of doing this.

You may simply write down all the details of your request and keep this either on your person or in your wallet or purse. I know many people who use talismans of this sort. If you are concerned that someone else might find your talisman and read what you have written, there are three options: One, you might write your request using a magical alphabet, such as Theban. Two, you might choose to describe your request in one or two words. Or three, you may further reduce these one or two words to a single number using numerology, as described in chapter 1.

For instance, if your request was to attract the right person into your life, you might simply write down the word *love*. Each time you look at this word on your talisman, it will bring back to your mind the complete request. I have used this method myself, and know that it works extremely well.

However, you might have specific reasons why you do not want anyone to see even the single word you have written on your talisman. In this case, you need to turn this word into a single number using basic numerology. In this instance, the word *love* would become the number nine. If anyone else happened to see the number nine written on a piece of paper, it would mean nothing at all. However, every time you looked at your talisman and saw the number, you would immediately be reminded that it was the numerological equivalent of the word *love*, and then the rest of your request would immediately come back to you.

You can write your message down on anything you wish. A piece of paper is probably the most convenient, as it can be folded and kept in a pocket, purse, or wallet. You may prefer to use parchment paper, or even make your paper. The effectiveness lies in the talisman, not in how it is made. Do not worry if you have no artistic skills. An artist might write the message in the middle of a beautiful decoration, but simply writing down the number on a scrap of paper will prove equally as effective.

Talisman for Health

Many people consider the word *abracadabra* to be a nonsense word used by children's entertainers. Actually, it has a long and fascinating history. No one knows exactly where the word came from originally, though it is probably derived from the Chaldean phrase *"Abbada ke dabra,"* which means "Perish like the word."[10] The words were first recorded by the Roman physician Quintus Serenus Sammonicus in 208 C.E., but they are believed to be much older than that. The talisman for "abracadabra" consists of eleven lines. The top row contains the word *abracadabra*. The next line eliminates the final letter, and a letter is dropped in each row until the bottom row contains simply the letter *A*.

```
ABRACADABRA
ABRACADABR
ABRACADAB
ABRACADA
ABRACAD
ABRACA
ABRAC
ABRA
ABR
AB
A
```

In the Middle Ages this talisman was used as a cure for fevers. The message was written on a piece of paper which was tied around the patient's neck with a piece of flax and worn for nine days. At the end of that time, the message was thrown backwards over the patient's shoulder into a stream that flowed east.[11]

If you are feeling unwell, draw this talisman on a sheet of paper and carry it with you for nine days. Read each line of the talisman out loud every day. As the letters decrease, so will your illness.

Traditionally, the writing of this talisman had to be done by someone who was pure of heart. It was important that the individual letters did not touch each other. It is also believed that this talisman is more effective when written in Hebrew letters. This is because *abracadabra* is written in nine letters in

Hebrew. Nine has always been considered a special, magical number.[12] Aleph, the first letter of *abracadabra* in Hebrew, is repeated nine times as the spell is spoken, and this also gives additional power to it.

A mystical word, such as *abracadabra*, that is engraved on a talisman is known as a *sigil.* (A sigil is also a magical shape; see below.) *Abracadabra* has stood the test of time. Other sigils that were popular in the Middle Ages are now virtually unknown. *Agla* was a popular sigil at one time. It was created from the first letters of the Latin phrase meaning "Thou art mighty forever, O Lord." The sigil *anizapta* was used to prevent drunkenness.

The names of Caspar, Melchior, and Balthazar, the three kings of the Christmas story, were used as a sigil to help find lost objects. The names were inscribed onto wax tablets and placed under a pillow. It is believed that they would produce a dream that revealed where the lost object could be found. Many people believed that this sigil could locate lost friends as well as misplaced items.[13]

Astrological Talismans

The origins of talismanic magic are lost in the mists of time. Ancient carved figures have been found dating back to Paleolithic and Neolithic times, showing that the practice goes back into prehistory.[14]

Astrological talismans are also extremely old, and are related to the seven planets that were known to the ancients. Each planet exerts its own character and influence on anyone who owns a talisman relating to a specific planet. Astrological talismans are usually magic squares (known as *kameas*) or sigils (a magical shape that contains the essence of a word).

A magic square is an arrangement of numbers in which every horizontal, vertical, and diagonal row add up to the same total. Magic squares have been used in many parts of the world for thousands of years, but their golden age, as far as magic is concerned, was in medieval times when such famous magicians as Abbot Johannes Trithemius (1462–1516) and Cornelius Agrippa (c.1486–1535) were active.

The best time to construct a magic square is during the hour or day that relates to that particular magic square. For instance, if you are wanting to receive the effects of Jupiter (wealth, honor, prestige, and health), you should construct a kamea of Jupiter during one of the hours or days of Jupiter.

Days and Hours of Saturn

The days and hours of Saturn are good times in which to write magic that relates to possessions or to business success. It is also a good time for learning of any sort.

Days and Hours of Jupiter

The days and hours of Jupiter relate to wealth, honor, prestige, success, self-improvement, and health.

Days and Hours of Mars

The days and hours of Mars are good times in which to write magic that relates to physical activity, power, and courage.

Days and Hours of the Sun

The days and hours of the Sun are good times in which to write magic that relates to friendship, good fortune, legal matters, personal reputation, and dissolving antagonism from others.

Days and Hours of Venus

The days and hours of Venus are ideal for friendship, love, family matters, beauty, and the arts. They are also good for travel.

Days and Hours of Mercury

The days and hours of Mercury are good times for writing magic that relates to communication, the intellect, learning, and diplomacy.

Days and Hours of the Moon

The days and hours of the Moon are good for travel, love, family matters, women, animals, and messages from overseas.

Planetary Days of the Week

Each of the seven planets rules a specific day of the week. In fact, this is how some of them they received their names in the first place. For instance, *Sunday* is derived from *Sun-day,* and *Monday* comes from *Moon-day.*

Sunday — Sun
Monday — Moon
Tuesday — Mars
Wednesday — Mercury
Thursday — Jupiter
Friday — Venus
Saturday — Saturn

Planetary Hours

The arrangement of planetary hours was devised in medieval times and divides the day and night into equal twelve-hour periods. In actuality, each planetary hour will not necessarily contain sixty minutes. In summer, for example, the daylight hours will be longer than sixty minutes, while the nighttime hours will be less.

To work out the planetary hours you will need to obtain charts of the sunrise and sunset times for the location you are in. My daily newspaper provides these for me. If they are not recorded in your local paper, you may be able to obtain them from the weather service or from a local synagogue. (Synagogues use them to determine the commencement and conclusion of their holy days.) Make sure that the times you find are correct for your location, as places that are only a one hour drive north or south of you will have slightly different sunrise and sunset times.

Once you have the sunrise and sunset times, you need to calculate the amount of daylight available. Divide this total by twelve to find out how long each planetary hour of daylight will be. For the nighttime hours you need to calculate the amount of time between the sunset of one day and sunrise of the next. Again divide this period of time by twelve to determine the exact planetary hours.

Figure 8.1 shows the planets that relate to each daytime and nighttime hour. If you are writing magic that relates to love, for example, you will want to do it either on a Friday or during any of the hours that relate to Venus. If your magic relates to money and finance, you will want to write your magic on a Thursday or during one of the hours that relate to Jupiter.

The Seven Kameas

The kameas for each planet are shown in Figure 8.2. They can be drawn on paper or parchment and carried as a talisman. If you have some particular purpose in mind, you will find it helpful to draw the specific kamea every day, as the act of creating it also sends your desire out into the universe. Think about your desire while constructing the kamea. Keep your thoughts positive, and remain confident that what you desire will occur.

DAYTIME HOURS

	Sunday	Monday	Tuesday	Wednesday	Thursday	Friday	Saturday
1	Sun	Moon	Mars	Mercury	Jupiter	Venus	Saturn
2	Venus	Saturn	Sun	Moon	Mars	Mercury	Jupiter
3	Mercury	Jupiter	Venus	Saturn	Sun	Moon	Mars
4	Moon	Mars	Mercury	Jupiter	Venus	Saturn	Sun
5	Saturn	Sun	Moon	Mars	Mercury	Jupiter	Venus
6	Jupiter	Venus	Saturn	Sun	Moon	Mars	Mercury
7	Mars	Mercury	Jupiter	Venus	Saturn	Sun	Moon
8	Sun	Moon	Mars	Mercury	Jupiter	Venus	Saturn
9	Venus	Saturn	Sun	Moon	Mars	Mercury	Jupiter
10	Mercury	Jupiter	Venus	Saturn	Sun	Moon	Mars
11	Moon	Mars	Mercury	Jupiter	Venus	Saturn	Sun
12	Saturn	Sun	Moon	Mars	Mercury	Jupiter	Venus

Figure 8.1. The Planetary Hours

NIGHTTIME HOURS

	Sunday	Monday	Tuesday	Wednesday	Thursday	Friday	Saturday
1	Jupiter	Venus	Saturn	Sun	Moon	Mars	Mercury
2	Mars	Mercury	Jupiter	Venus	Saturn	Sun	Moon
3	Sun	Moon	Mars	Mercury	Jupiter	Venus	Saturn
4	Venus	Saturn	Sun	Moon	Mars	Mercury	Jupiter
5	Mercury	Jupiter	Venus	Saturn	Sun	Moon	Mars
6	Moon	Mars	Mercury	Jupiter	Venus	Saturn	Sun
7	Saturn	Sun	Moon	Mars	Mercury	Jupiter	Venus
8	Jupiter	Venus	Saturn	Sun	Moon	Mars	Mercury
9	Mars	Mercury	Jupiter	Venus	Saturn	Sun	Moon
10	Sun	Moon	Mars	Mercury	Jupiter	Venus	Saturn
11	Venus	Saturn	Sun	Moon	Mars	Mercury	Jupiter
12	Mercury	Jupiter	Venus	Saturn	Sun	Moon	Mars

Figure 8.1. *(continued)*

133

KAMEA of SATURN

4	9	2
3	5	7
8	1	6

KAMEA of JUPITER

4	14	15	1
9	7	6	12
5	11	10	8
16	2	3	13

KAMEA of MARS

11	24	7	20	3
4	12	25	8	16
17	5	13	21	9
10	18	1	14	22
23	6	19	2	15

Figure 8.2. Planetary Kameas

KAMEA of the SUN

6	32	3	34	35	1
7	11	27	28	8	30
19	14	16	15	23	24
18	20	22	21	17	13
25	29	10	9	26	12
36	5	33	4	2	31

KAMEA of VENUS

22	47	16	41	10	35	4
5	23	43	17	42	11	29
30	6	24	49	18	36	12
13	31	7	25	43	19	37
38	14	32	1	26	44	20
21	39	8	33	2	27	45
46	15	40	9	34	3	28

Figure 8.2. *(continued)*

KAMEA of MERCURY

8	58	59	5	4	62	63	1
49	15	14	52	53	11	10	56
41	23	22	44	45	19	18	48
32	34	35	29	28	38	39	25
40	26	27	37	36	30	31	33
17	47	46	20	21	43	42	24
9	55	54	12	13	51	50	16
64	2	3	61	60	6	7	57

KAMEA of the MOON

37	78	29	70	21	62	13	54	5
6	38	79	30	71	22	63	14	46
47	7	39	80	31	72	23	55	15
16	48	8	40	81	32	64	24	56
57	17	49	9	41	73	33	65	25
26	58	18	50	1	42	74	34	66
67	27	59	10	51	2	43	75	35
36	68	19	60	11	52	3	44	76
77	28	69	20	61	12	53	4	45

Figure 8.2. *(continued)*

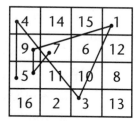

Figure 8.3. Sigil for Geraldine

Sigils

You have already learned that a sigil is a mystic word inscribed on a talisman. A sigil is also a design created by turning the letters of a name into numbers using numerology, and then creating a design by tracing a line joining each of these numbers. Let's assume that your name is Geraldine. Using the numerology chart in chapter 1, the letters become the following numbers: 7, 5, 9, 1, 3, 4, 9, 5, and 5. We can create a sigil of these numbers on any of the kameas, but for the purposes of this example, we will assume that Geraldine is wanting to be more successful in her life and chooses to create a sigil on the kamea of Jupiter. Figure 8.3 shows this.

Chinese Talismans

The Chinese have been writing their own magic for longer than anyone else, and their hand-written talismans (known as *fu*) are good examples of this. A fu is usually written on a sheet of yellow, black, or red paper, seven inches long by three inches wide. The writing is done using red or black ink. These talismans are mentioned in the oldest Chinese manuscripts and date back thousands of years. The Yellow Emperor, father of the Chinese people, is believed to have beaten Chih You at the Battle of Cholu because the Queen Mother of the West had given him a fu.[15]

Chinese talismans can be made out of any material, but are usually made from paper. On the paper a message is written to the spirits, usually asking the evil spirits to avoid harming the wearer of the talisman. Because the message is addressed to spirits, it is usually written in "ghost script," a strange form of Chinese that is understood only by Taoist adepts.[16] These talismans are either attached to the person's shoulder, back, or breast, or stuck to a wall of the person's house.

Pages from used calendars were often used as talismans. This is because the calendar was considered an essential, and extremely valuable, part of life. They were hung up over pigsties or burned. The ashes would then be mixed with the swill to act as a preventative against illness.

Incantations against demons were written on yellow paper which was burned. The ashes were mixed with water and then drunk to provide protection. This is known as the *shao hui t'un fu* ("the swallow ashes charm"), and is an interesting example of writing your own magic. Spells to cure people suffering from various illnesses were written on leaves or paper. These were then burned and the ashes mixed with liquid, which the patient drank. This is known as "drinking holy water."

Religious talismans are made from narrow slips of red or yellow paper. These contain sacred words and are usually attached over doorways and on the walls of houses, though some are worn, while others are burned and swallowed.

All-purpose amulets, possibly showing the eight trigrams from the I Ching or a few words that wish the bearer good luck, are commercially available.

The Chinese New Year is the most important day in the Chinese calendar. On this day, old paper talismans are removed and replaced with new ones. Five pieces of paper are stuck above the front door, on trees, furniture, and anything valuable, to represent the "five happy things" (wealth, longevity, peace and quiet, virtue, and good health). Paper money is burned to send wealth and prosperity to the person's ancestors. Nowadays, paper items such as television sets, cars, houses, and even beer cans are frequently burned as well to ensure that life is happy on the other side.

Shopkeepers write the words *lucky* or *fortunate* on pieces of paper which they place in the drawers of their desks. Frequently, they are pasted in position. This is another good example of writing your own magic. Of course, these words also act as affirmations as well as talismans.

The Chinese New Year is the best time to pass out *angpow*, the famous red envelopes containing "lucky money." Married people and employers normally give these to the young and single. In return, the young and single give wishes for a long and prosperous life. The real money in the red envelopes can be used to pay bills at any time of the year. In fact, payments due to others are often handed over in a decorated red envelope.

In February 1986, a fu was used to help solve a case of embezzlement at a branch of the Bank of Taiwan in Kaohsiung. While the police were still working on the case, two of the bank employees consulted a local *chitung* (shaman) named "Red Boy" to see if he could help solve the case. After thinking about the matter for some time, Red Boy asked the bank employees to bring one of their coworkers to see him. To ensure that she did come, he gave them a fu to attach to a leg of her chair. This person came to see Red Boy and confessed to the crime.[17]

There are apparently more than a million types of fu available, covering every possible type of request that anyone could ever need. For instance, there are fu that relate to every possible computation of health, wealth, love, and happiness. There are also fu for protection while travelling, fu that can change your fate, fu that help you locate lost items, and fu that enable children to be spanked by their parents without feeling pain.

Farmers make use of many types of fu to protect their animals, ward off insects, mice, and snakes, attract rain, prevent disasters (man-made or natural), and to ensure a profit at the end of the season.

A proper fu is blessed by a Taoist priest before use, and the incantation he chants is extremely important. The words he chants and the words on the fu are inseparable. After the blessing, the fu is usually twirled around a joss stick three times and given to the person to use. Because of the large number of requests for fu, many temples have the more common types of fu mass-produced by printing machines to keep up with the demand.

New Year Scrolls

Another important part of the Chinese New Year are the scrolls that are displayed on front doors to welcome the spring and to attract prosperity. Since ancient times, people, no matter what their status in life, have used these scrolls to display their literary skills or to express their desires and hopes for the future. Although the tradition began much earlier, scrolls did not become popular until the Ming dynasty (1368–1644) when Chu Yuan-chang decreed that everyone had to attach a New Year's scroll to their doors.

The subject matter of these scrolls vary. Many simply welcome the start of spring. Farmers may hang scrolls wishing for peace and harmony amongst their animals. Some contain aphorisms and words of advice, such as "Goodness is a jewel that flows down to one's descendants; forbearance is the way to the fortune virtue brings," or "All men are brothers within the four seas; look after others as well as your own family." Others might advertise the type of business they are engaged in. And, of course, many are aimed at attracting greater success into the home. "Every day a pound of gold," "Welcome good fortune from all four seasons," and "Calling on wealth, visit us here," are all examples.

Nowadays, most scrolls are mass-produced and contain clichéd messages. However, it is still a matter of pride to write a poetic couplet that is fresh and different, and also relates to the family's desires and needs.

Many scrolls today also contain just a single character such as *spring, wealth,* or *good fortune.* These are usually hung upside down because "upside down" is, in Chinese, a homonym of "to arrive." Hanging the message upside down signifies the arrival of spring.

Obviously, the Chinese are more open than Westerners when it comes to writing their own magic. I cannot imagine a home in the West with the words "Calling on wealth, visit us here" attached to the front door. However, in their own way the Chinese people are magnetizing themselves. They compose the message, write it down, and then display it for all to see.

Every time they see this message or affirmation, it becomes more and more embedded in their consciousness, and as we all attract to us what we think about, they are likely to achieve their goals.

Show Your Gratitude

While you are waiting for your request to be answered, give some thought as to how you will express your gratitude to the universe. Thank the universe in advance for granting your request. Decide exactly what you are going to do to express your gratitude. The more you give of yourself, the more you will receive in return. Give abundantly and you will receive abundantly. This giving may bear no direct relationship with your request, but it is still a form of expressing your gratitude to the universe for giving you what you want.

Write Your Own Magic with Crystals and Gemstones

Chapter 9

Sermons in stones, and good in everything.

WILLIAM SHAKESPEARE (1564–1616)

IN THE PREVIOUS CHAPTER you saw how powerful amulets and talismans could be in attracting to you whatever you want. It is also possible to use crystals and gemstones in your home to achieve the same effect.

People have been aware of the incredible power of crystals for thousands of years. Crystal energy has been used for many purposes such as curing illnesses, developing intuition, providing protection, cleansing and balancing chakras, divination, meditation, and attracting whatever we want.

The ancient Egyptians created beautiful jewelry that was intended to improve the quality of life of the wearer. For instance, Galen recorded that the Egyptian king Nechepsus wore an amulet of green jasper carved into the shape of a dragon. This was placed over his digestive organs to strengthen them. The results were extremely beneficial.[1] Incidentally, it is said that Galen himself also wore a ring containing jasper to staunch blood.[2]

In addition, the ancient Chinese wore beautiful jewelry on acupuncture points to provide protection and increased energy. And according to the Bible, the high priests put on a breastplate containing valuable gemstones when they wanted to communicate with God.[3]

The magicians, seers, and wise men of the past attributed gemstones with many qualities that they deduced from observation and experimentation. For instance, gemstones are related to the different planets, the signs of the zodiac, and different qualities, ranging from virtues to health. It is quite possible that people began wearing precious stones for talismanic reasons long before they began using them to beautify themselves. It is sad that today jewelry is used mainly for adornment.

I first learned how to use crystals and gemstones to attract whatever I wanted to me when I was in Hong Kong. My late friend who lived there, Tai L'au, always had something interesting to teach or show me. He was a natural teacher with an engaging method of imparting information. He was a slight man with an infectious laugh. Everything amused him, and I think it was his sense of humor that kept him healthy and active until his sudden death at the age of ninety-three.

"You want to learn?" he'd ask me, with a laugh.

"Yes, yes," I'd reply. "That's why I'm here."

"You not here to see me?" His English was remarkably good, but he amused himself by speaking in pidgin English when he taught.

"Of course I'm here to see you, but I want to learn as well."

"What you want to learn?"

"About crystals and gemstones."

"Ah." Tai L'au would hug himself and rock to and fro. "Precious stones. You want wealth?" Then he would laugh uproariously, as if he had made a wonderful joke.

Time meant nothing to my master. It made no difference to him if a lesson took five minutes or five hours. However, he never let a lesson finish until he was sure that I had absorbed everything I needed to know.

"Why is dollar bill green?" he asked.

"I have no idea."

Tai L'au would shake his head. "That's no answer. Think. Why dollar bill green?"

"Does green relate to money?"

I knew I was on the right track when Tai L'au started laughing.

"Yes, yes," he said, when his laughter finally stopped. "Green is the color of wealth. Find a green crystal to hold when you meditate. Hold in your left hand. You'll be wealthy man if you do." Then he laughed again. "Yellow works too." He shook his head. "But green is better."

It may not have been an orthodox method of teaching, but I can still recall many lessons verbatim. I can't say that about any other teacher I have learned from.

On my next visit to Hong Kong I took Tai L'au some greenstone, a particularly beautiful jade that comes from New Zealand. He was thrilled with the gift and rocked to and fro with it clasped firmly to his chest. I knew that he was psychometrizing the jade as he rocked to and fro.

"Why you bring me this?" he asked.

"You told me that green is the color of wealth. I wanted to bring you something green."

"I not need wealth." He looked around his tiny apartment. "I have everything." He thought this a huge joke and laughed for what seemed like minutes.

"You told me that green meant wealth in all ways, not just money."

Tai L'au nodded his head. "You learn. Good boy." Then he laughed again.

Later he told me that the best crystal for attracting financial wealth was a green pyramid-shaped crystal. He cautioned me, however, to never use it for purely selfish goals. Rather, I was to think about how I could use all the wealth I created to help others, as well as myself.

"Remember the price," he said. "There's always a price to be paid."

I was interested to discover later that he regularly used green crystals whenever he sent out a personal request to the universe. The method he taught me is commonly used in the East. I have seen it practiced in Hong Kong, Malaysia, Singapore, the Philippines, Indonesia, Sri Lanka, and India. Still, it appears to be little known in the West.

Tai L'au's Seven Crystal Ritual

Tai L'au's ritual uses the familiar Star of David which consists of two equilateral triangles, one pointing up and the other down (Figure 9.1). The best dimensions are those using either seven or eight. A Star of

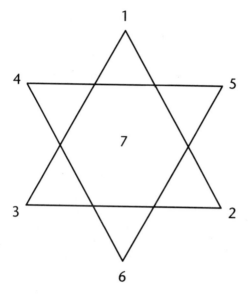

Figure 9.1. Star of David

David that has sides of seven or eight inches (or centimeters) will be more powerful than one with sides of any other length.

You will need six small gemstones and one that is at least twice the size of the others. It is best if they are all the same color, but you can use a variety of colored crystals or gemstones if you wish. I have a set of green stones that I use.

It is important that you find the stones or crystals attractive and enjoy handling and looking at them. Do not rush out and buy the first stones that you find. Take your time. Handle the stones and see what feelings you receive when you hold them. Some stones appear warm, others cool. Some appear to tingle in your hand. Others may create an effect in another part of your body. Take your time, and pay special attention to the stones that react to your touch.

Cleansing

Naturally, the stones will need to be cleansed before use. There are several ways of doing this. If the stones are new, you should bury them in rock salt for three to four hours. This removes any vibrations they may have received from former owners. After removing them from the salt, wash your stones in clean, prefer-ably running, water and allow them to dry in the sun-shine. Once they are dry, polish them gently with a clean cloth, and they are ready for use. Dispose of the salt, as it will have absorbed all of the negativity from the crystals and should not be used again.

Whenever you can, wash your crystals in rainwater. If this is not possible, use cold tap water. While wash-ing the crystals fill your mind with thoughts of love. Suggest that all harmful and negative energies leave the crystal, leaving only positive energies behind. Think about your desire in a positive, expectant manner. All of these feelings will be transmitted into the crystal.

You can also cleanse your crystals by placing them on a cluster of amethyst or clear quartz for at least twenty-four hours. Before using them, hold them in your hands and fill them with thoughts of love.

Another method is to bathe your crystals in the light of the sun or the moon. Place them in a window where they will receive as much good energy as possible.

Many people find that burying their crystals in the ground for twenty-four hours is a good way of cleansing and recharging them. Bury any terminated crystals with their points downward. Wipe them clean with a cloth when you uncover them, and sense if they are ready for use.

Finally, you can cleanse your crystals and gemstones by holding them in your right hand, closing your eyes, and sending thoughts of love to them. Relax as much as possible, and visualize yourself surrounded by a clear, white, purifying light. Feel this light entering your body through the top of your head and going down your right arm to your hand and the stone.

After cleansing, if the crystals are wet, allow them to dry naturally, ideally in direct sunlight. Once they have dried, polish them gently with a clean cloth. After this, place the six smaller stones into position on each point of the Star of David. There is a set way of doing this. The first crystal is placed on the topmost point of the upward-pointing triangle. The second crystal is placed on the bottom right-hand side of the same triangle, and the third crystal is placed on the remaining point of this triangle. The fourth crystal is placed on the point of the downward-pointing triangle that is immediately above the third crystal. The fifth crystal is placed on the point to the right of the fourth crystal, and the final small crystal is placed in the very bottom position. The seventh crystal, the large one, is then placed in the center of this formation.

This arrangement can now be activated to provide good luck for you and everyone living in the house. This is done by visualizing the arrangement of crystals as a vortex of energy that rises upwards in a spiral. Many people find it easier to visualize this if they look directly down on the crystals until they can imagine the energy moving around and around in a circle. They then move back and allow the energy to spiral upward.

Naturally, the crystals need to be looked after. Dust them regularly and wash them whenever necessary. Since crystals absorb thoughts and vibrations, wash them as soon as possible after harsh words have been spoken in their vicinity. If you have been involved in the altercation, wait until you feel calm and relaxed so that you can fill the crystals with thoughts of love while you clean them.

This Star of David will provide protection and good luck for your home and everyone living there. You can, however, also use it for much more specific purposes. To do this, you will need a photograph of yourself that was taken when you were smiling or laughing. It is important that you look happy and that the photograph shows no one else but you. On the back of this photograph write down whatever it is that you want, but write it as if you already have it. In other words, write it as an affirmation. If your request relates to money, for instance, you might write, "I have five thousand dollars in the bank." You may have no money at all in the bank at the time you write down this request, but that does not matter. If you wish to conceive, you might write, "I have a beautiful baby daughter/son," depending on what you want.

Attach this photograph to the large, central crystal in the Star of David. Visualize the swirling energy spiraling upward from the Star of David and out into the universe, ultimately to bring you whatever it is you have requested.

Mandalas

Chapter 10

A single word, even, may be a spark of inextinguishable thought.

PERCY BYSSHE SHELLEY (1792–1822)

 MORE THAN THIRTY YEARS AGO, I was taught what I believe to be the greatest secret in writing your own magic. The man who taught it to me was a minister in the Presbyterian Church of Scotland. I wasn't aware of it at the time, but I realize now that he was a rebel in many ways. He healed people by the laying on of hands. Many people inside the church did not approve of this, but because he was successful, he was allowed to continue his healing ministry. Healing was one thing. Magic was something else entirely. He must have trusted me greatly to share this secret with me.

He began by showing me a book of symbols and logos. Many of them were familiar to me.

"Isn't it interesting," he said, "that you can look at a simple symbol and instantly be reminded of what it represents? This shows the deep, intrinsic connection between the two. An appropriate symbol or logo becomes, in effect, what it represents. If I was to show you a symbol of a football team, you would immediately be transported to the team's home ground in your imagination."

He passed me a sheet of paper and a pen. "Now quickly, without even thinking about it, draw me a simple design that represents your home." When I hesitated, he added, "Don't think about it. Just do it. Quick, quick."

I hastily drew a picture of a house and a garden. My friend shook his head. "I don't want a picture. I want a symbol. It might be two strokes with the pen, it might be a hundred. Okay?" He turned the paper over. "Do it now. Quick, quick."

This time I drew something without thinking. It turned out to be an egg-shaped outline with some wavy lines inside it. It took perhaps twenty seconds to draw.

My friend looked at it for a long time, silently nodding his head. After a long pause he asked me to tell him about it.

"Well," I began. "The egg represents home and family. Safety, I guess you could say. Security and love. The lines inside represent my family."

"Why are they intertwined?"

"To show that our lives are intertwined. What one person does has an effect on all the others."

"And what does it make you feel?"

"Make me feel?" I was surprised at the question. I had no idea that my childlike drawing was supposed to make me feel anything.

"Yes. Look again, and tell me what you feel."

I did as he suggested, and to my surprise, all sorts of emotions came to the surface.

"I feel warmth, love, sadness that I'm so far away from home, tenderness—is that enough?"

He clapped me on the back. "That's good. Tell me, if you lost that picture and suddenly found it again ten years later, would you still get the same feelings?"

"They might change slightly, but they'd still be feelings about home and loved ones."

"Exactly!" My friend beamed with delight. "That squiggle can be your symbol for home."

I still had no idea what my friend was teaching me. However, over the next several evenings he encouraged me to draw many other symbols depicting a variety of emotions.

Although I did not know it at the time, I was drawing mandalas. A mandala is a geometric representation of the cosmos and usually consists of a series of concentric circles around a central point that symbolizes the universe.[1] The central point, known as a *bindu,* is a focal point for meditation. A formal mandala has three basic qualities: a center (bindu), symmetry, and cardinal points. Of course, in a circular mandala the cardinal points are not visible, even though they are still present.

In its simplest form, a mandala can be a mere dot. It contains the essential bindu, perfect symmetry, and the cardinal points. A mere dot is complete in itself and represents God. Of course, your drawings will usually contain much more detail than this. Drawing a bindu on a sheet of paper is usually just the starting point of the mandala.

Yantras are a type of mandala that are constructed for meditative purposes. In effect, a yantra is a picture of the divine, and consequently has to be treated with reverence.[2]

A pictorial yantra is usually constructed from circles, triangles, squares, and lotuses. Mandalas are traditionally made from circles and squares. The circle has always been considered a symbol of the psyche, or the self. Even Plato described it in these terms.[3] The square symbolizes the earth, the body, and the everyday world.

We need not be constrained by these limitations. The drawings we produce are simply pictures from our heart that represent and depict the thought or emotion we are expressing. There are many examples of abstract mandalas. The rose windows found in many cathedrals are good examples, as are the halos surrounding Jesus and the saints in many religious paintings. Circular mandalas even appear in rock engravings that predate the invention of the wheel.[4] Modern-day examples can be seen in the ground plan of Washington, D.C., and the work of such contemporary artists as Paul Klee, Wassily Kandinsky, Robert Delaunay, and Paul Nash.

When creating your own mandalas it is helpful to start with a dot, and then build a design around it while focusing on whatever it is you are depicting. Draw quickly and with as little conscious thought as possible.

You can choose any subject at all. I have a set of twenty designs that depict a variety of subjects. I originally drew these on sheets of 8½ x 11–inch paper. This is a good size to display on a wall. I also wanted a smaller set, so that I could carry around with me any particular card or cards that I was focusing on at the time. I originally copied the designs onto blank business card stock, but I found a deck of blank-faced playing cards in a stationery store. These are an ideal size to carry in my wallet or pocket.

My designs are black and white, but there is no reason why you should not do them in color if you wish. You may choose to do the designs in different colors, or color in your finished design. Do not choose the colors logically. Again, let your intuition guide you as to the correct colors to use.

You can draw designs to cover any subject you wish. The topics in my set of cards are:

love
spirituality
meditation
my wife
my children
my grandchildren
happiness
home
friends
career
goals
study
writing

health
money
travel
retirement
creativity
hopes and dreams
public speaking

Your set of pictures may be completely different. One of my students compiled a set of designs that included:

avoiding illness
attracting a partner
overcoming insomnia
eliminating evil spirits
contacting her guardian angel
making friends
gaining a pay increase
avoiding Alzheimer's disease

As you can see, there is no limit to the designs you can draw. The only thing that matters is that the subject of the design is important and relevant to you. You do not need to prepare twenty designs. One or two might be all that you need. I prepare new ones as and when I need them. These usually relate to specific goals. Some become a permanent addition to my collection of designs, while others are used until they have served their purpose and are then discarded.

How to Use Your Symbols

The symbols are drawn from your heart and depict topics that are of great importance to you. Consequently, they possess incredible power at a subliminal level. Every time you look at your symbols, changes occur below the level of conscious awareness.

I prefer to hang the symbol I am working with on the wall of my office. I have a special frame for my symbols, and anyone seeing them probably thinks that they are rather weird examples of modern art. Hanging the symbol on the wall means that I see it frequently and it becomes a silent affirmation. Every time I see it I am reminded of my purpose for having it on display. No one else knows what it is, or what I am displaying it for. At times, people comment on my symbols, but they have no idea of their true purpose.

The symbols are easy to use. At least once a day, sit in front of your symbol with your eyes at the same height as the bindu, or central point, of the drawing. Gaze into the center of the drawing for at least a minute. This imprints the entire design on your subconscious mind.

Gradually start to think about your purpose for drawing the symbol. If it is a goal, think how your life will be once your goal has been realized. Imagine that the goal has already been achieved. Feel the sensations of success and happiness in your body. Maintain this sensation for as long as you can.

165

Finally, close your eyes and give thanks to the universe for granting you your request. Open your eyes and look at the design again. Stand up and bow toward the symbol, acknowledging its role and thanking it for making your dreams come true. Once you have done this, continue with your day. You will feel relaxed and positive after this exercise.

In the East, it is believed that when you meditate on a mandala, you first perceive it as a map of the world. It gradually transforms itself to symbolize you, and then ultimately, as you continue to meditate, it depicts you in perfect unity and balance with the cosmos.

Mandala of Protection

We all need protection at times. Although we might think that we can handle anything that life throws at us, we all gradually become worn down and weakened by such things as stress, a difficult boss, the negativity of others, or a psychic attack. The constant accumulation of small frustrations can gradually build and ultimately destroy our well-being. Many heart attacks have been attributed to stress and tension in the workplace.

Fortunately, we can eliminate these tensions from our lives by drawing a symbol of protection. Start by placing a bindu in the center of a sheet of 8½ x 11–inch paper. The paper should have the long side facing you so that it is in a landscape position, rather than a portrait one.

Place your hands in a relaxed position on the paper with your thumbs touching each other beneath the bindu. Notice where your little fingers lie. Draw a small circle at the places where the tips of your little fingers rest.

Close your eyes and think about your need and desire for protection. Once you have done this, open your eyes again and, as quickly as possible, draw a design that depicts your feelings of protection. The only requirement is that the design incorporates the two circles where your little fingers rested.

You have now created a mandala of protection. You can use it whenever you feel the need for protection, or want to eliminate the stresses and pressures of life. It can also provide energy if you feel overtired or listless. Be careful when using it for this purpose, though. This mandala creates unlimited energy. If you have been overworking, it is better to rest rather than give yourself more energy so that you can continue to work.

All you need to do is place your mandala on a table, rest your hands on it with the thumbs touching and the tips of your little fingers in their circles. By doing this you are creating a circle of protection that includes your chest, arms, hands, and thumbs. This in itself is protective and gives feelings of security. However, you are also gaining the protective power of the mandala. The symbol you drew provides enormous additional power that enters your body through your little fingers. In effect, this is creating a second circle of protection that runs from one thumb across the back of your hand to your little finger, and across your symbol to the little finger of your other hand, on to the back of your hand and thumb, where it all starts again.

The incredible power of your special symbol, created by your heart and subconscious mind and combined with two circles of protection, has to be experienced to be believed.

Working in a Group

Chapter 11

Words, when written, crystalize history; their very structure gives permanence to the unchangeable past.

FRANCIS BACON (1561–1626)

 THERE ARE ADVANTAGES and disadvantages to writing magic entirely on your own. Obviously, you would not want to write extremely personal requests in front of others, but many requests are greatly enhanced when performed by a group. Examples are requests that benefit others. You might send out a request to help a community, town, country, or even the world.

Over the years, I have been involved in a number of master mind groups. This is a term devised by Andrew Carnegie and popularized by Napoleon Hill, the celebrated author of *Think and Grow Rich*. Hill spent many years studying the success habits of the most successful people of his day. Most of them were involved with small groups of like-minded people who provided encouragement, advice, and acted as a sounding board for ideas.

There was a psychic element as well. Hill found that whenever two people got together they "created a third, invisible, intangible force which may be likened to a third mind."[1] In other words, when two people work together with the same aims in mind, they have the potential to create much more than two individuals working on their own.

Dion Fortune (1891–1946) was a prolific author and the founder of the Society of Inner Light. She dedicated her whole life to reviving the Mystery Tradition of the West. In her book *Applied Magic and*

Aspects of Occultism, she referred to the master mind group as "the Group Mind."[2] She believed that when a group of people worked together for a common goal they created an artificial elemental being. This being has a power of its own that encourages every member of the group and gives them telepathic powers. The more the group focuses on the ultimate goal, the larger the elemental becomes, further inspiring every person in the group.

The eminent occultist W. E. Butler (1898–1978) agreed with this when he wrote: "In the magical workings of a lodge, constructive visualization is practiced, and definite 'thought forms' are created."[3] A good magical lodge is an excellent example of a powerful master mind group.

Your group can be any size you wish. Andrew Carnegie's master mind group consisted of fifty people. Large numbers are helpful if your goal is universal in scope. Napoleon Hill explained that Mahatma Gandhi, in effect, created a gigantic master mind group of more than two hundred million people that worked and cooperated together in a state of harmony to achieve a worthwhile goal.

The master mind groups I have been involved in have all contained between four and six people. Your group may contain more or less than this. There are no hard-and-fast rules. Most people are able to find a small number of like-minded people who will work with them to achieve a common goal. But choose your group carefully. It is much better to have a strong group of two people, than a divided group of three or four or more. I have seen groups destroyed because one or two of the members had their own aims that were at odds with the goals of the rest of the group. Avoid people who are dishonest, half-hearted, listless, or apathetic. You need enthusiastic people who are prepared to contribute to the group and make a difference.

Oddly enough, I have found that busy people are usually the best choice. These people are usually enthusiastic, vital people who willingly put their energies into anything they believe in. People who are ambling through life, doing as little as possible to get by, lack the energy and motivation required to keep a master mind group alive.

Once you have found your group, you will need to organize regular meetings. Someone will have to chair the meetings to keep them on track and ensure that they don't disintegrate into casual conversations. In the groups I have been involved in, we have always taken turns acting as the chairperson.

Naturally, you will have to discuss your particular goal and phrase it in words. You might find it helpful if all members write down their requests at home and bring them to the meeting. Even though you all want the same thing, everyone will have phrased it differently and will have a slightly different slant on the subject. This all needs to be discussed and clarified until finally you have a specific goal that pleases everyone. All members of the group should write down this goal and take it home with them to think about until the next meeting.

At the next meeting, any questions anyone has should be addressed. The wording may have to be changed slightly. Certain parts of the request may not be clear to everyone.

Once questions are out of the way, the members should discuss their goals again, this time focusing on the benefits that will occur once the request has been granted. This is intended to motivate and inspire the group to action.

Finally, each member of the group has to write out the request again and send it out into the universe. It is better to make a formal ceremony of this rather than have it as part of a regular meeting. If the weather is good, I prefer to burn the papers out-of-doors. When a group I was involved in were concerned about the future development of a certain piece of land, we conducted a ceremony one evening on the actual site.

The papers can be burned separately or together. With a master mind group of four people, each person can stand at one of the cardinal points and burn the papers in a north, south, east, and west order. Alternatively, the members of the group can stand in a circle and set fire to all of the papers at the same time.

The ceremony needs to be conducted seriously, but it can be fun. You are allowed to laugh and celebrate the fact that your request has gone out into the universe and will shortly be granted. Laughter contains incredible power, and I often think that many ceremonies are far too solemn and serious.

After the burning ceremony, the group will have to continue to meet to discuss progress and to keep everyone motivated and enthusiastic. It is generally easier to magnetize a group in this way than it is for an individual working alone. We are all prone to doubts and negative thinking at times, and the positivity of a group can help enormously.

If your group has gathered together for one single aim, you may decide to disband once the goal has been achieved. This can be hard if you have worked for a long time on a large-scale goal. However, you may have discovered other goals that you can work on as a group, and, as long as everyone is eager, your group can stay active indefinitely. Still, be prepared to let go of this particular master mind group once it has achieved its aims. There is no point in hanging on to something that no longer serves any useful purpose. You can always create another master mind group when necessary.

Casting Spells

Chapter 12

Words are, of course, the most powerful drug used by mankind.

RUDYARD KIPLING (1865–1936)

BEING ABLE TO write your own magic makes it particularly easy to cast spells for any purpose you desire. Whenever we make magic, we influence the universal energies to achieve our goal. We do exactly the same when we cast a spell.

We can cast a spell for any purpose, good or bad. However, you are asking for trouble if you cast an evil spell on someone else since the law of karma will return the harm to you. So make certain that your spell will hurt no one, directly or indirectly. As the saying goes, "If it harm none, do what ye will."

Neither can you cast a spell for something that is impossible for you. If you are a forty-five-year-old, overweight smoker, it is a waste of time sending out a spell that will make you an Olympic champion sprinter.

If the spell is not right for you, it will not be granted. Usually, we know inside ourselves that something is not right for us. However, we may persevere because of a financial need or to live up to the expectations of others. You may ultimately be successful at activities of this sort, but you will never feel completely happy or fulfilled, and the price you have to pay will usually be far too high.

If you are not sure if a particular spell is right for you, sit down quietly somewhere and ask yourself the question. Sense how the particular goal feels inside you. Imagine what your life will be like once the goal has been accomplished. Ask yourself if you are prepared to pay the price. If you do not feel a spark of excitement inside you when you think about the goal in this way, think carefully before sending out your request.

Essential Requirements

The Four Elements

Spells make use of all four elements: air, fire, water, and earth. These primordial elements are considered the universal forces and have a vital role to play in spell casting. Each of these elements provide their particular attributes and strengths to help send your spell out into the universe. The particular items that are used to represent the elements vary according to the type of spell. A candle usually represents the fire element. Crystals or flowers and plants satisfy the requirements for the earth element. Water may well be the water in the bowl containing the flowers. Air can be provided by a small fan, or even the sound of your own voice.

Timing

The different phases of the moon are extremely important for the success of your spells. In the past it was believed that evil spells were cast during the time of the waning moon, when it is moving from full to new. Constructive, or positive, spells were cast during the waxing moon, as it grew from new to full. It is doubtful if this was ever the case, but today we use all phases of the moon when casting spells. The waxing moon is the best time to perform spells that relate to abundance, expansion, and growth. The waning moon is the best time to cast spells that relate to decreasing, diminishing, or vanishing. It is also a good time to cast spells that can help us eliminate any negative thoughts or feelings.

Days of the Week

Each day of the week has a special relevance, as you learned in chapter 8.

> *Sunday* relates to the Sun and the color gold. It is a good day for casting spells relating to love, universal peace, advancement, healing, and spirituality. It also relates to the father.

> *Monday* relates to the Moon and the color silver. It is a good day for casting spells relating to peace, pregnancy, creativity, and intuition. It also relates to the mother.

> *Tuesday* relates to Mars and the color red. It is a good day for casting spells relating to strength, health, vitality, passion, protection, and leadership.

> *Wednesday* relates to Mercury and the color yellow. It is a good day for casting spells relating to knowledge, communication, and self-expression. It is also a good day for spells that draw clients to you.

Thursday relates to Jupiter and the color green. It is a good day for casting spells relating to work, career, financial matters, expansion, excitement, and success.

Friday relates to Venus and the color pink. It is a good day for casting spells relating to love, romance, friendship, and beauty.

Saturday relates to Saturn and the color blue. It is a good day for casting spells relating to patience, self-discipline, responsibility, and standing up for yourself.

It can be frustrating to decide on Monday that you want to cast a spell to help you find a lover, and then have to wait until Friday to do it. In fact, the delay is good in magical terms. You will frequently be thinking about your purpose in sending out this spell between Monday and Friday, and this strengthens the request in your mind. When you make your spell it will have much more power and energy behind it.

The planetary hours (chapter 8) indicate the best hours in which to send out your spells. Naturally, it is better to cast spells in the nighttime hours, as magic is always much stronger in the dark. I have cast spells in the daytime and had good results, but there is a distinct loss of atmosphere when casting spells in the full light of day, and I believe that this can affect the final result.

Your Spell

The spell that you cast is your particular goal at this time. You can compose this in any form you wish. Spells seem to work best if they are written in the form of rhyming couplets. It makes no difference if they are serious or humorous. I tend to prefer light-hearted spells, as I believe that magic should be fun, even when the intent is serious. Here are some examples of spells I have used:

"Becky's gone and hurt her knee,
We want it better, don't you see?"

"Money has been hard to find,
Kindly help us ease this grind."

"Somehow Rachel's lost her keys,
Help us find them, pretty please."

"Mike and Sarah want a baby,
Give me a yes, not a maybe."

"Jeffrey's gone and caught the flu,
Cure him quick—I don't like him blue."

As you can see, all of these are lighthearted, even though each request is basically serious. I find that the effort involved in creating a rhyming couplet makes the spell much more effective than it would have been if I had simply taken a standard spell from a spell book. It also makes it extremely easy to remember and recite while casting the spell. Naturally, in each case there is much more to the spell than is revealed by the couplet. The couplet synthesizes and condenses the ideas behind the spell. You can, if you wish, write down absolutely everything that is involved in the spell, and then burn that. However, that is not necessary, and it is also hard to recite.

This is not to say that spell books should not be used. They serve a definite purpose, and I have compiled my own spell book which I use from time to time. One of the advantages of using a spell book is that you do not have to think much about the process, and can instead put your energies into thinking about the positive outcome. All you need to do is gather the right ingredients, intone the right words at the right time, and wait for your spell to be granted.

Many people have told me that they find it impossible to write rhyming couplets. The spell does not have to be written in this way. You can write it in any form you wish, but avoid formal-sounding writing. Write your spell as if you were telling a good friend about it. This automatically eliminates the "thees" and "thous" that I hear from time to time.

The spell can be written on any type of paper. In one sense, it does not matter what you use, as it will be burned anyway. However, I like to write my spells on good quality parchment paper. I find this aesthetically pleasing. This is also why I write my spell on the paper with great care and try to make it look as neat and attractive as possible. I am sure the spell would work if I merely scribbled my request down on a scrap of paper, but I feel better for having made an effort. Also, I am sure that the time I put into choosing the right paper and writing the spell is not wasted, as I am thinking about my request the whole time.

Altar

You will need an altar where you can place the various items that are used in a spell. Some people have a special altar, but this is not essential. Part of the kitchen table is fine. I am fortunate to have the large stump of a tree to use as my altar when working outdoors. Cover the altar with a cloth. This can be any color you wish. Most people choose red, white, or black, but there is no reason why you cannot have a different color if you wish. Avoid synthetic material. As well as the specific items that are required for your spell, you can also place on your altar anything that has special meaning for you.

Candles

We have already discussed candles in chapter 7. It is better to use beeswax or vegetable fat candles when spell casting. Sometimes the color of the candle is decided by the day of the week or the spell that is being cast. At other times the color can be determined by personal choice or by using numerology or astrology.

Candles are often used to symbolize a certain person. In these instances, it is helpful to use a candle that relates to this person's sign of the zodiac.

> Aries—red
> Taurus—blue
> Gemini—yellow
> Cancer—violet
> Leo—orange
> Virgo—dark blue
> Libra—green
> Scorpio—dark red
> Sagittarius—purple
> Capricorn—dark green
> Aquarius—bright blue
> Pisces—pale green

Herbs

Common herbs play an important role in spell casting. Many spell casters grow their own herbs, but they are easily obtained in both fresh and dried form from gourmet food and health food stores.

Suggested herbs are given with the following different spells. However, there are countless substitutes that can be be used in preference, or as an alternative. These are listed in Appendix B.

Crystals

Crystals have a major role to play in many spells. They can be used to symbolize a person, or for their own intrinsic magical power. Crystals absorb our energy patterns and reflect them back to the universe. They raise our conscious awareness, enabling us to achieve more than we ever thought possible. They can clear our minds and thus enable us to focus on what we really want. They can also eliminate negative energies. Consequently, we use crystals to add power to any spell or ritual.

Incense

Incense has been used in religious ceremonies for thousands of years. It is believed that gods enjoyed the perfume, but evil spirits found it distressing and stayed away. Also, the smoke produced helps carry the requests up to the gods.

It is entirely up to you whether or not you wish to use incense in your spell casting. There are four basic types to choose from: loose, cone, cylinder, and stick. Loose incense is by far the easiest to make, but if you are buying commercially made incense, obtain it in cylinder or stick form, as they last the longest. You can choose incense that relates specifically to the type of spell you intend to cast (see Appendix B). Alternatively, you may decide to use a particular incense simply because you happen to like it.

Procedure

Naturally, you will have to procure the items that are required for the particular spell you are casting. Place these on your altar. Light your candle and sit comfortably in a position where your eyes are in direct line with the flame.

Close your eyes and take ten deep breaths, holding each one for a few moments before exhaling slowly. Relax yourself as much as you can. When you feel totally relaxed, open your eyes again and gaze at the candle. Think about the spell you are about to cast. In your mind's eye see yourself performing the various elements of the ritual. Visualize the energies going out into the universe. Finally, see yourself as you will be once the spell has been granted. Visualize it as clearly as you can. Some people see an actual picture in their minds. Others see very little, but experience it in other ways. As long as you can imagine a successful outcome, you are visualizing correctly. It makes no difference how you sense this, just as long as you can feel the success in your body.

Now it is time to perform whichever spell you have chosen. Once the spell is completed, sit down and again visualize yourself enjoying the successful outcome of your spell casting. Visualize this for as long as you can before carrying on with your life.

Visualize the successful outcome every time you have a few spare moments. You will experience doubt and negativity at times, but whenever you notice that you are thinking in this way, switch your thoughts around and make them positive. After all, the universe wants you to have what you desire. Your spell will be granted as long as it is in your best interests.

The spells described here are examples only. You can use them as written, but you will have better results if you think about them and make any changes that will personalize the spell for you and your needs. This is especially the case if you write your own personal couplets since they then become imbued with your spirit. Make the couplets as detailed as possible. Mention specific names and dates. To activate the air element, read the couplets out loud.

When blowing the ashes into the four cardinal directions, I've found it is easiest to do this by dividing the remaining ashes into four piles and placing them on the palm of your hand one at a time. Also, it is preferable to use your fingers or a candle snuffer to put out a flame. Some people say that you should never blow out a candle while performing any ritual. However, when you are working outdoors, you will find that the wind does this all the time. If you do not have a candle snuffer and dislike the idea of snuffing it out with your fingers, simply blow the candle out.

Spells for Love

Throughout history, there have been more spells cast to attract or keep love than every other type combined. It is sad that so many people are living without love, or are inside a relationship but do not feel happy or secure. Fortunately, we can cast spells to attract love to us, and to keep love alive.

Spell to Attract an Unknown Lover

Best day: Friday.
Candle: Pink.
Herb: Cinnamon.

Smear the sides of your candle with honey and place it in the center of your altar. Sprinkle the cinnamon around the candle. Place a glass of water on the right side of the altar. Place a small metal or ceramic dish in front of the candle.

Light the candle, relax, and meditate. Think about the qualities you want in your lover. Write the following couplet on a sheet of paper.

"For far too long I've been alone and free,
Please guide my lover safely home to me."

Read the couplet out loud and then burn the sheet of paper in the flame. Once it is fully alight, place it in the dish in front of the candle. Watch it burn and say the couplet out loud five more times. Then, think about your purpose in making the spell while you watch the candle burn.

Pick up the container holding the ashes. Drop a few ashes into the glass of water. Gently blow the remaining ashes into each of the four cardinal directions.

Finally, drink the glass of water containing the ashes and put out the candle.

Spell to Attract a Certain Person

Best day: Friday.
Candle: Pink, or color that relates to the other
person's horoscope sign.
Herb: Cinnamon.

You need to be careful with this spell. You will be wanting a certain person to become your lover, but you need to be certain that the other person feels the same way about you. It is black magic to use this spell on someone who does not desire you.

Smear honey around the sides of the candle. Sprinkle sugar and cinnamon onto the candle. Place this in the center of your altar. Place a glass of water on the right-hand side of the altar, and a small metal or ceramic dish in front of the candle.

On the left hand side of the altar place something that belongs to the person you are intending to attract. This could be an item of clothing or some small object that the person has handled recently. A photograph of the person works just as well. Alternatively, you can draw a picture to represent the person. Strands of hair taken from a hairbrush or nail clippings also work well.

Light the candle and think about your reasons for performing this spell. Write the following couplet:

> "My heart desires [*name of person*] with unfailing devotion,
> Bring him/her to me for lifelong love and passion."

Read the couplet out loud and then burn it. Place it in the dish. Place your left hand on the object owned by the person you desire and say the couplet out loud five times.

Gaze into the candle flame and think of your future with this person. Kiss the object, and then place a small amount of the ashes into the glass of water. Blow the remaining ashes in each of the four cardinal directions.

Finally, drink the water and put out the candle.

Spell to Increase Passion

Best days: Friday and Sunday.

Candle: Five red candles, plus a candle that relates to your partner's zodiac sign. You can inscribe your partner's name onto this candle if you wish.

Herb: Cinnamon.

Crystal: Any red crystals, plus a crystal that relates to you and another that relates to your partner. These crystals are those that relate to your zodiac sign or month of birth (see chapter 8).

Sadly, passion gradually slips away from many relationships. Here is a spell to help revive the passion.

Arrange the five red candles in a semicircle at the back of your altar. Smear the candle that relates to your partner with honey, and sprinkle it with cinnamon. Place this in the center of the altar. In front of this place a metal or ceramic container to accept the ashes from your spell. On the right side of the altar place a glass of water.

Place the crystals that relate to you and your partner at the front of the altar. Place the additional red crystals in a semicircle to meet the red candles and create a complete circle.

Light all six candles. Meditate and think of your need for more passion in your life. Imagine you and your partner making passionate love for hours on end. Write down the following couplet:

"Unlimited passion is what I seek,
I want to have it now, not next week."

Say it out loud. Light the piece of paper on fire and place it in the container while it still burns.

Gaze into the candle flame. Picture how your life will be once it is full of passion again.

Complete the ritual by placing some of the ashes in the glass of water and blowing the remainder in the four cardinal directions. Drink the water, and put out the candle, starting with the red ones and finishing with the candle that symbolizes your partner.

Spell to Release a Lover

Best day: Saturday, preferably with a waning moon.

Candles: One white candle, plus two additional candles, to depict the two people involved. Use zodiac signs to determine the correct colors to use.

Herb: Myrtle (this herb promotes love and peace).

Crystal: Agate or quartz crystal (to promote healing).

Relationships do not always last forever. If it is time for a relationship to end, there is nothing to be gained by hanging on. Some spells cause harm to the person you are releasing. This spell allows you to release your lover, without causing unnecessary pain.

Place the two candles that represent you and your partner in the center of your altar. The candle depicting the male should be on your right as you face the altar. Place a small metal or ceramic container in front of these candles to contain the ashes. Place the white candle in a central position behind the other two candles to create a triangular formation at the rear of the altar.

Place the myrtle in the center of your altar at the front. Place the crystals on both sides of the altar. If you are using just one crystal, place it behind the myrtle and in front of the candles.

Light the candles that symbolize you and your partner. Meditate quietly for a while and think about the good times the two of you have enjoyed. Write down the following:

"We had laughter, love, and good company,
But now it's time for us both to be free."

Set fire to the paper, lighting one end from one of
the candles and the other end from the other. Drop
the burning paper into the container while repeating
the couplet over again and again.

Once the paper has turned into ashes, close your
eyes, and in your imagination see yourself setting
your partner free. Experience the sensations you will
feel in your body. When you feel ready, say out loud,
"Goodbye."

Put out the two candles, and lay them on their
sides. Pick up the white candle using both hands. Say
out loud, "I am free, I am free."

Light the white candle and place it in the middle of
your altar. Gaze at the flame and visualize the purity
and goodness of the white candle entering you, making you whole and free.

Drop a pinch of ashes into the glass of water, and
blow the remainder in the four cardinal directions.
Drink the glass of water, and finally, put the candle out.

Spell to Discourage Unwanted Attention

Best day: Saturday. (Sunday is also satisfactory, if
the unwanted person is male. Monday can be used,
if the unwanted person is female.) The moon
should be waning.

Candle: One small, light blue candle.

Herbs: One teaspoon each of chili powder, black
   pepper, and paprika.
Photograph: A photograph, caricature, or drawing
   of the person being discouraged.

It can be difficult when someone you do not want to
become involved with finds you appealing. You may
already be happily involved in another relationship,
or you may simply not find this person attractive. It
makes no difference what the reason is, you simply
want that particular person out of your life. Here is a
spell that enables you to discourage these unwanted
advances, without hurting the other person.

Mix the chili, pepper, and paprika together. Coat
the photograph with oil on both sides, and sprinkle it
with some of the herbs. Wrap it in newspaper or a
cheap, dark-colored cloth. (A photograph is best for
this particular spell, but you can still perform the
spell by drawing a rough representation of the person. This might even be a stick figure with the person's name written underneath it.)

Place the wrapped photograph on a large plate and
place this at the front of your altar.

Light the candle and gaze into the flame as you think
of your need to be free from this unwanted attention.

Sprinkle the rest of the herbs in a circle around the
plate containing the photograph.

Write down the following couplet:

"I know you mean well, but you're not for me,
Goodbye—I'm not part of your history."

If you have written your own couplet, make sure
that the person's name is included in it. This adds
extra power to the spell. Burn the piece of paper
while saying the couplet out loud. When the paper
becomes too hot to handle, drop it onto the plate containing the photograph. (You do not want to set fire
to the photograph or its wrapping. Be prepared to
slap out the flames if necessary.)

Wait until the candle has burned itself out, and
then pick up the plate containing the photograph and
the ashes. The purpose of the plate is twofold: You do
not want the photograph to desecrate your altar, and
it also enables you to avoid handling the photograph
and its wrappings.

Dispose of the photograph and its wrappings in a
public trash bin. As you drop it in, say "Goodbye"
with as little emotion in your voice as possible.
Wash the plate thoroughly in boiling water before
using it again.

Spells for Success

Most people want to be more successful than they
already are. We all want more love, more money, better health, and so on. Here are some spells to help
you become more successful in these key areas.

Water of Abundance

Waters with magical properties have been used for thousands of years. They are easy to prepare. Place a few crystals of amethyst, sapphire, or turquoise into a bottle. Fill the bottle with water that has been filtered or boiled. This creates a symbiotic reaction. The crystals give their particular energies to the water, which, in turn, purifies the crystals.

Drink a glass of this water every morning and again in the evening. Fill up the bottle with additional water every evening. As you drink, visualize prosperity and abundance reaching out into every area of your life.

There is an additional benefit from preparing water of abundance. The crystals gain enormous power and energy. Carry one of the crystals around with you at all times to attract additional wealth. Change the crystal you carry with you every day.

It is helpful to drink a glass of the water of abundance before performing any of the following rituals.

Spell for More Money

Best day: Thursday, waxing moon.
Candle: Green.
Herb: Clover.
Crystal: Zircon.

Inscribe the exact sum of money you desire onto your candle. Inscribe your name below this figure. Dress your candle with olive oil and place it in the center of your altar. Place a metal or ceramic container in front of the candle, and a glass of water to your right. Sprinkle the clover in a circle around the candle.

Light the candle and gaze into the flame while thinking about your need for additional money. Place the zircon in your right-hand palm. Rest the back of this hand on the palm of your left hand. If you are not using zircon, use the largest coin you can find. A half-dollar will work well, but an overseas coin that is larger in circumference would be even better. It does not matter what denomination the coin is since its role is purely symbolic. Think of what you would do with your additional money and how your life will improve once you have it.

Place the zircon (or coin) on the altar to your right. Write down the following couplet:

> "Money is needed urgently,
> I want it now, please come to me."

If you are writing your own couplet, include the exact sum of money you desire. For instance, if you needed ten thousand dollars, you might write:

> "I need ten thousand dollars, preferably today,
> I need it urgently, please bring it right away."

Read the couplet out loud three times. Then burn it while reciting the couplet another three times. Say the couplet twice more as you watch the last of the paper burn away. The couplet is said out loud eight times in total. (The number eight relates to money in numerology.)

Distribute the ashes into the glass of water and the four cardinal directions and say "Thank you" out loud as you do so. Pick up the zircon (or coin), toss it into the air, and catch it again as it falls. This symbolizes wealth coming to you from heaven. Finally, drink the water and put out the candle.

Repeat this ritual once a week until the required amount of money arrives. You can use the same candle each week, but it must be dressed each time before you use it.

Spell for Prosperity

Best day: Thursday, waxing moon.
Candle: One each of gold, red, green, and purple, plus one that relates to your zodiac sign.
Herb: Basil.
Crystal: Turquoise.
Also required: One horseshoe-shaped magnet.

Prosperity comes in many forms. This spell will attract prosperity to you in every sense of the word.

Place the candles in a semicircle on your altar with the candle that symbolizes you in the middle. Immediately in front of this candle place the magnet with its legs pointing toward your candle. In front of this place a metal or ceramic container for the ashes. To the right of this place a glass of water. Place a sprig of basil on top of the magnet. Finally, drop the turquoise into the glass of water.

Light the candles in order, starting with the one furthest to your left. As you light each one, say out loud, "I deserve abundance." Say it as enthusiastically as you can.

When all the candles have been lit, sit in front of them and think of the abundance you desire in your life. Imagine yourself living abundantly. See how happy and carefree you are.

When you feel ready, write the following couplet on a piece of paper.

> "I have so much abundance in every part of my life,
> I've done away with poverty, limitations, and strife."

Burn the piece of paper while repeating the couplet out loud. Drop the burning paper into the container, and think how blessed you already are, and how much richer you are going to become.

Place a few of the ashes into the glass of water, and blow the remainder in each of the four directions. Put out the candles, from left to right. Drink the water. Allow the turquoise to dry naturally.

Carry the magnet and turquoise with you for at least a week, even when you have a bath or shower. If you have not noticed any changes in that time, repeat the ritual.

Spells for Protection

There is a common saying that the only people who do not suffer from stress are in graveyards. Of course, some stress is good as it motivates us to get things done. This type of stress is known as *eu-stress*. Bad stress, known as *dis-stress*, can be produced in many ways. Difficult relationships or lack of a relationship, shortage of money, abusive situations, unemployment, psychic attack, and even someone cutting you off on the freeway contribute to bad stress.

Fortunately, we can protect ourselves against the effects of bad stress and any other negative situation by creating a spell of protection.

Protection Spell

Best day: Tuesday.

Candle: Red (a white candle, or one that symbolizes your sign of the zodiac, can also be used).

Herbs: Anemone, angelica, borage, dill, parsley, sage, and thyme.

Crystal: Amethyst or jade.

To prepare, inscribe the words "I am protected," followed by your signature, on the candle. Grind and mix the seven herbs together and keep them in a sealed container.

When you are ready to start, place the candle in the center of your altar. In front of this place a metal or ceramic container to hold the burning paper. To the right of this place a glass of water. In the same position on the left-hand side of your altar, place the crystal.

Sprinkle the herb mixture in a circle around your altar and ensure that it surrounds the candle, container, water, and crystal. Create a larger circle by sprinkling herbs in a circle around your altar and the area where you will sit.

Sit inside this circle and light the candle. Gaze at the flame and think of the changes that will occur in your life once you feel totally protected. Visualize yourself totally surrounded by a circle of white light that penetrates every part of your body. Allow pleasant feelings of relaxation to drift through you.

When you are ready, write the following couplet on a sheet of paper.

"I am protected. I feel safe and calm.
Nothing can hurt me. I'm shielded from harm."

Stand up and face north. In a strong voice, repeat the couplet. Turn around to face the south and say the same words again. Repeat with the east, and finally the west.

Sit down and set fire to the paper, saying the words out loud once again. Place the burning paper in the container.

Wait until all that remains is ashes. Close your eyes and give thanks to the universe for protecting you. Picture yourself surrounded by a shield of white light. Hold this image for as long as you can, and then open your eyes.

Place a pinch of the ashes into the glass of water. Stand up and blow the remaining ashes to each of the four directions. Drink the water and put out the candle.

Repeat this ritual whenever you feel it necessary.

A Talisman Protection Spell

Best days: Saturday or Sunday. Moon must be waxing.
Candle: Orange.
Herbs: Basil.
Crystal: Amethyst or green jade.
Incense: Incense is desirable for this spell. Choose something that you find pleasant.

We can add strength to a talisman by using it in a spell. Many talismans are designed purely for protective purposes, and one of the most famous of these is a magic square made up of letters. It is described in the *Key of Solomon*,[1] one of the early magical grimoires, and dates back to at least the first century C.E. Examples of magic squares were found in the ruins of Pompeii.[2] The following is a magic square made up of letters bearing a message that can be roughly translated as, "Sator, sower of the seed, spins the wheel."

To prepare, obtain a piece of black cardboard, approximately four inches square, and a marking pen that writes in gold ink. You will also need some silk to wrap the cardboard talisman in after the ceremony. Black, red, violet, and gold are all suitable colors. Alternatively, you can use the color that relates to your zodiac sign.

When you are ready to begin, place the candle in the center of your altar. Immediately in front of this place a saucer containing ground basil. Place a glass of water on the right-hand side of the altar, and the crystal on the left. Place the cardboard immediately in front of you, with the pen beside it.

Light the candle and sit in a comfortable position facing it. Think about your need for protection. Close your eyes and imagine yourself surrounded in pure white light. Hold this image for as long as you can.

Open your eyes and draw the following magic square on the black cardboard:

SATOR
AREPO
TENET
OPERA
ROTAS

This magic square can be read horizontally and vertically, as well as backwards and forwards. Draw the magic square slowly and carefully, concentrating on each movement of the pen, while thinking of your need for protection.

When you have finished drawing the magic square, hold it in your right hand and pass it through the smoke of either the candle or the incense eight times. Recite the words on the magic square as you do this.

Replace the magic square on the altar and put the crystal on top of it. Say the following couplet:

"I am safe and protected from all sorts of harm,
I am grateful and vow to look after my charm."

Close your eyes and think how much better your life will be now that you are protected. When you are ready, open your eyes and hold the magic square in your left hand. Dip your fingers into the glass of water and allow a few drops to fall on to the magic square. Drink the water and wrap the magic square in the piece of silk while saying "Thank you" out loud.

This magic square has now become a powerful talisman of protection. It has been consecrated by the elements of fire, earth, air, and water, and is ready to serve you for as long as you need it. Carry it with you wherever you go. Every time you see it, give silent thanks for the protection it is providing.

Spells for Work

Most of us spend a great deal of time at work. We can use spells to find a job, and to make our working environment more pleasant. We can cast spells to help us get on better with the people we work with, and to make us more productive.

Spell to Find Work

Best day: Thursday, with a waxing moon.
   Wednesday can also be used.
Candle: Three are required: orange, purple, and one to symbolize you. If you are looking for your first paid job, choose a white candle to represent you. Otherwise, use a candle that relates to your sign of the zodiac.
Herb: Chamomile and clover.
Crystal: Clear quartz or amethyst.

Place the three candles in a semicircle at the rear of your altar. The candle that symbolizes you should be in the center. Place a glass of water on your right-hand side, and the crystal on your left. Place a metal or ceramic container for the ashes immediately in front of the candle that represents you. Place the herbs in a circle that encompasses everything on your altar.

Light the candles while silently giving thanks for all the blessings you already have. Rest your hands on your thighs, palms up. Close your eyes and meditate for a while. Think of your need to find work.

Decide on the specific position you would like to have, and visualize yourself already doing it. Be as specific as possible. If you have a particular company in mind, imagine yourself working there.

Write the following couplet on a piece of paper.

"I need a job, and I need it right away.
Lead me to the perfect job I need today."

Read the words out loud three times. Then burn the paper, lighting it with the candle that symbolizes you. Drop the ashes into the container. Wait until the fire has gone out and then close your eyes and give thanks to the universe for leading you toward the position you want.

Open your eyes again. Sprinkle a few ashes into the water, and blow the remaining ashes into each of the four directions.

Put out the candles in the following order, orange, purple, and finally yours.

Repeat once a week until the right position is offered to you.

Spell to Make Work More Enjoyable

Best days: Wednesday or Thursday.

Herb: Three leaves from a lime tree (leaves from a lemon tree also make an effective substitute).

Crystal: A dark-colored crystal.

Also required: One small bell and a couple of ounces of earth.

Ideally, this spell should be cast as close to your working area as possible. If you work at a desk, use that as your altar. If you work in a factory, you may have to improvise. An upturned box or a chair can work perfectly well as temporary altars.

It is possible to conduct this ritual with other people around, but it is better to do it entirely on your own. Obviously, your working conditions dictate whether or not this is possible.

Hide the leaves in your work area. You might place one under a potted plant, another in a drawer, and the third under a rug. It does not matter where you hide them, just as long as they are out of sight. Take the earth and sprinkle it under your desk or in the area where you work.

Write down the following couplet.

"I enjoy my work, and its getting better every day,
I get along well with everyone, and work's
   becoming play."

Place it on your desk. Hold the crystal in your left hand and the bell in your right. Ring the bell once, and recite the couplet out loud. You can whisper it, if need be.

Fold the piece of paper into quarters and keep it with you for ten days. On the tenth day burn it wherever you happen to be. Repeat the couplet as the paper turns to ashes. Blow the ashes into each cardinal direction.

Spell for a Job Promotion

Best day: Thursday.
Candle: Green.
Herb: Clover.
Crystal: One that relates to your zodiac sign (see chapter 8).

To prepare, inscribe words on the candle that relate to your desire for a promotion. If you have a specific job in mind, inscribe that on the candle. Alternatively, inscribe "I am progressing upward" on the candle. Sign your name on the candle also.

When you are ready to begin, place the candle in the center of your altar. Sprinkle clover leaves around it. In front of the candle place a metal or ceramic container for the ashes. Light the candle, and sit comfortably in front of it. Hold the crystal in your right palm. Rest the back of your right hand on your left palm.

Close your eyes and think about your work, and your desire for a job promotion. Think about the different things you will do at work to ensure that the promotion occurs.

Open your eyes, place the crystal on the left-hand side of the altar, and write the following couplet.

"I'm working hard to achieve success,
I'm happy and proud of my progress."

Read the words out loud. Fill your mind with thoughts of your upward progress, and then burn the paper. Drop the burning paper in the ashes container and repeat the words several times as the paper burns.

When the flames cease, close your eyes and give thanks to the universe for giving you the talent and ability to progress in your chosen career.

Lick the tip of your right forefinger and dab it in the ashes container. Rub the ashes into the center of your left palm. Repeat with your left forefinger. Rub your palms together and say the couplet out loud once more.

Take the rest of the ashes and blow them to each of the four cardinal directions.

Repeat once a week for as long as necessary.

Spells for Each Day of the Week

You will find spell casting stimulating and exciting. It can also be extremely addictive, and you may find yourself wanting to cast spells every day of the week. If you do this, choose a topic that will benefit others. You may cast spells for worldwide peace, or to help oppressed people in different parts of the world. A friend of mine casts spells regularly to help save whales. She has also cast spells to help save the rain forests. It makes no difference what your goal is, as long as it is designed to help other living things.

The basic format stays the same every day. However, the color of the candle depends on the day of the week.

Sunday—gold
Monday—silver
Tuesday—red
Wednesday—yellow
Thursday—green
Friday—pink
Saturday—dark blue

Place the candle in the center of your altar. Place a metal or ceramic container immediately in front of it to hold the ashes. On your left-hand side place a crystal that relates to your sign of the zodiac (see chapter 8). On your right-hand side place a glass of water. Light the candle and meditate on your reasons for casting this spell.

There is a different magic square for each day of the week (see Figure 8.2). Construct the correct magic square slowly and think about your spell as you do so.

When the magic square is completed, hold it up high in the air and ask the universe to help you achieve your goals. Wait until you feel a sense of peace and calm in your body. Set fire to the magic square and deposit it in the ashes container.

Quietly meditate. Send out your feelings of love and concern. Visualize them surrounding your altar and then spreading out to ultimately encompass the entire world.

Stand up. Place a small pinch of ashes in the water. Face north and drink about a quarter of the water.

Repeat with south, east, and west. Finally, blow the ashes to each of the four directions.

You can cast spells for any purpose. Spell casting is a personal business and you should do it in a way that feels comfortable for you. A friend of mine always says the Twenty-third Psalm out loud, before and after each of her spells. It feels right for her, and therefore plays an important part in all of her rituals. Many people say a mantra while casting spells. I have seen countless people repeating a chant over and over again, gradually increasing in intensity and volume as the spell progresses. Other people prefer peace and quiet, and speak out loud only when absolutely necessary. A former neighbor of mine, on the other hand, always conducted his rituals with heavy metal music in the background. This would not feel right for me, but it was perfect for him.

Some people cast spells in an almost cold and emotionless manner. Others become overcome with emotion and pour out their feelings of love and concern. Again, there is no right or wrong way. Express your emotions if you feel like it. Keep them hidden if that is what you want.

Your rituals can be as short or as long as you wish. The best time to stop is when you feel that you have successfully visualized the outcome, and can feel a sense of "knowingness" inside you that the spell is going to work. Some people enjoy lengthy rituals.

Others prefer them to be as brief as possible. Again, it is entirely up to you.

You can cast spells with other people, if you wish. Naturally, everyone must have the same goal in mind. The results that can be obtained with group spells is incredible. Spell casting lends itself well to a master mind group.

The most important thing in spell casting is to constantly remain aware of your purpose in conducting the ritual. This is essential for positive results. I have seen people become so involved in the drama and theatricality of their rituals that they forget entirely why they were doing them. Needless to say, they did not achieve the results they were looking for.

Like everything else, practice is required. In time, the spells develop a rhythm of their own, and you will find yourself completely relaxed as soon as you start. You will also derive enormous pleasure and satisfaction as your spells create for you the life you desire and deserve.

Afterword

The pen is mightier than the sword.

EDWARD BULWER-LYTTON (1803–1873)

By now you will be aware of the enormous benefits that writing your own magic can bring to your life. I have seen many people, including myself, totally transform their lives as a result of following the procedures in this book.

Now it is up to you. Study and learn as much as you can about magic. Start with small goals. Watch what happens. Once you become successful with small goals, move on to larger ones.

Remember though, that writing down your own magic does not mean that it will miraculously happen. You cannot rely entirely on magic. You have to play your part as well. The harder you work, the "luckier" you will become. Combine writing your own magic with hard work, and you will be amazed at the results.

Finally, do it. Nothing will happen unless you decide what you want, write it down, send it out to the universe, and magnetize yourself. Everything you need to know to write small magic, large magic, and anything in between, is in this book. You might want to cast a spell to make a new friend, or you may want to create a ritual that will change the world. Make up your mind to do it, and then write your own magic. I wish you great success.

Appendix A

Suggested Progressive Relaxation

Use this progressive relaxation only if you find it hard to relax. As you gain experience, you will stop needing to use a relaxation tape. However, like me, you may choose to use one every now and again, simply as a change.

Feel free to change these words so that they flow easily for you when you say them out loud. Say the script out loud a few times before recording it on tape. Record the tape in a pleasant, relaxed manner. Some people make extremely serious-sounding tapes for themselves. There is no need for this. You should speak slightly slower than usual, and allow a slightly longer pause than usual between sentences. The script that follows is about six minutes long.

Take a nice deep breath in, and close your eyes as you exhale. Allow a wave of pleasant relaxation to drift right through your body. Each breath you take makes you relax deeper and deeper. It is so pleasant to relax, without a care in the world. Nothing to bother or disturb you, just this pleasant feeling of relaxation drifting into every pore of your body.

Each breath you take makes you more and more relaxed, more and more relaxed. Take three deep breaths now, holding each breath for a moment or two before you exhale. One, breathe in. Feel that wonderful oxygen coming into your lungs. Hold it for a moment, and then exhale slowly. That's right. Nice, deep breaths. Two, breathe in. And as you exhale feel the sense of relaxation in your body. Three, breathe in. Hold it, and then exhale slowly.

You are becoming more and more relaxed with each breath you take. Feel that relaxation drifting into your big toes now. They may even tingle as they feel that pleasant relaxation. Allow that sense of relaxation to drift into all of your toes. That's good, that's very, very good. Allow the relaxation to drift into every part of your right foot and up to your ankles.

When you feel it happen, allow the same relaxation to drift into your left foot.

Allow it to drift over your ankles, and into your calves and knees. Relax more and more with each breath you take. Allow that relaxation to drift into your thighs, and up, up into your abdomen.

Pause for a moment and become aware of your breathing. Notice that you are breathing slowly, steadily, and evenly, and realize that each breath is allowing you to relax deeper, and deeper, and deeper.

The lower half of your body is now completely relaxed. What a wonderful feeling to be so totally relaxed. Allow that feeling of relaxation to drift up into your chest now, and up, up into your shoulders. Let it float down your arms, relaxing more and more, right down to the tips of your fingers.

And now, allow the muscles in your neck to relax. Once they have let go, allow that feeling of relaxation to drift into your face, your eyes, and up to the top of your head.

You are relaxed all over now, from the top of your head right down to the tips of your toes. It is a wonderful, pleasant feeling, but you can go even deeper into this wonderful, peaceful, tranquil state.

Imagine yourself now standing on a deck, overlooking a beautiful garden full of gorgeous, multicolored, sweet-smelling flowers. In the distance are tree-covered hills and the pleasant scent of pine comes delicately to you. The sky is a vibrant blue, and a couple of fluffy clouds are gamboling happily in the warmth of the beautiful day. You can see some birds high up in the sky. Their happy sounds as they call to each other bring back happy memories of relaxing vacations in the past.

There is a staircase leading from the deck down to the garden. You feel a strong desire to go down the steps and walk amongst the flowers. You place your hand on the handrail and look down the staircase. There are ten steps. Ten wooden steps that appear to have been fashioned by a talented craftsman. The grain of the wood creates beautiful patterns of texture on the steps.

As you count from ten down to one allow yourself to double your relaxation with each step you take, so that by the time you reach the freshly mown grass at the bottom you'll be totally, absolutely, completely relaxed in every muscle and fiber of your being.

Ten—double your relaxation as you take one step.

Nine—double your relaxation yet again.

Eight—drifting down, deeper and deeper.

Seven—so calm, so relaxed, so, so peaceful.

Six—double your relaxation yet again.

Five—halfway down now. Feel that relaxation in every fiber of your being.

Four—deeper, deeper, and still deeper.

Three—smelling the flowers now as you double your relaxation yet again.

Two, and one.

As you step off onto the beautiful lawn and look around you, it feels as if the grass is removing every last trace of tension from every part of your body. You walk over to a beautiful comfortable seat and sit down, revelling in the beauty and tranquility of the scene. You feel more relaxed than you have ever felt before, and each breath you take continues to take you deeper, and deeper, and deeper.

So calm. So peaceful, and so, so relaxed.

If you feel completely relaxed by the time you sit down on the comfortable seat, you are ready to continue with the ritual. If you still feel tension anywhere in your body, simply carry on with the scene for a while longer. Get up from the seat, walk across the freshly mown lawn, and find another set of steps to take you down to another, deeper level of this magnificent garden. Count from ten down to one again as you descend these steps and find a pleasant spot in the sun in which to sit and enjoy the tranquility of the scene.

You may need to do this a number of times when you first start experimenting. With practice, however, you will find it becomes easier and easier, and you will be able to shorten this relaxation stage considerably.

Do not worry if it takes you longer than you think it should to relax. Everyone is different, and some people find it easier than others. The ability to relax can also vary from day to day, depending on how difficult or easy the day has been. Simply take however long it takes and enjoy the process.

Appendix B

Herbs for Different Purposes*

Herbs for Love

Allspice

Almond

Angelica

Anise

Balm of Gilead

Basil

Bergamot

Bindweed

Caraway

Cassia

Catnip

Cherry

Cinnamon

Cinquefoil

Cloves

Coriander

Dill

Elder

---

*Do not ingest these herbs. Some may be harmful or fatal if swallowed.

Fennel Ginger
Ginseng
Honeysuckle
Jasmine
Juniper 🖐
Lavender
Lemon Balm
Lemon Verbena
Lilac
Maidenhair
Marigold
Marjoram
Mistletoe 🖐
Motherwort
Mustard
Myrtle
Nutmeg
Orange
Oregano
Peppermint 🖐

Plantain 🖐
Poppy
Primrose
Rose
Rosemary
Sage
Southernwood
Spearmint 🖐
Star Anise
Strawberry
Sunflower
Tarragon
Thyme 🖐
Valerian
Vervain
Violet
Willow
Wisteria
Yarrow 🖐

Herbs to Heighten Sexual Desire

Almond
Anise
Basil
Bay
Bergamot

Calamus
Caraway
Cassia
Celery
Cinnamon

🖐 Handling in fresh form may cause contact dermatitis.

Cinquefoil

Cloves

Coriander

Damiana

Garlic

Ginger/Ginseng

Jasmine

Juniper 🤚

Lavender

Lovage

Maidenhair

Mandrake 🤚

Musk

Mustard

Myrtle

Nettle 🤚

Nutmeg

Onion

Orchid

Parsley

Peppermint 🤚

Rose

Rosemary

Sage

Sarsaparilla

Spearmint 🤚

Tarragon

Turmeric

Vervain

Violet

Wormwood 🤚

Herbs for Happiness and Well-Being

Basil

Borage

Dittany

Jasmine

Lemon Balm

Lemon Verbena

Marigold

Marjoram

Motherwort

Myrrh

Myrtle

Orange

Oregano

Parsley

Peppermint 🤚

Rosemary

Spearmint 🤚

Valerian

Herbs That Enhance Psychic Perception

Anise
Althea
Basil
Bay
Cassia
Cedar
Cinnamon
Cinquefoil
Cloves
Coriander
Dittany
Elder
Frankincense
Garlic
Hibiscus
Holly
Honeysuckle
Lavender

Lemon Grass
Lilac
Marigold
Mugwort 🖐
Nutmeg
Onion
Parsley
Poppy
Rose
Safflower
Sage
Sandalwood
Strawberry
Sunflower
Thyme 🖐
Willow
Wormwood 🖐
Yarrow

Herbs to Eliminate Negativity

Anise
Asafoetida
Basil
Bay
Broom
Cassia

Cedar
Cinnamon
Cranesbill
Dill
Elder
Eucalyptus

Frankincense

Garlic

Holly

Jalap

Lavender

Mistletoe ✋

Mugwort ✋

Myrrh

Onion

Peppermint ✋

Rose

Rose Geranium

Rue ✋

Sage

Sandalwood

Spearmint ✋

Thyme ✋

Valerian

Vervain

Willow

Woodruff

Yarrow ✋

Herbs That Aid Job Promotion

Basil

Borage

Catnip

Civit

Clover

Elder

Fennel

Garlic

Jalap

Marigold

Melilot

Menthol

Mustard

Onion

Orris

Pepperweed

Poppy

Safflower

St. John's Wort ✋

Slippery Elm

Spikenard

Storax

Sunflower

Tarragon

Turmeric

Yohimbe

Herbs for Confidence

Borage
Cranesbill
Fennel
Garlic
Mustard
Rose Geranium

Rosemary
St. John's Wort 🖐
Tarragon
Thyme 🖐
Turmeric

Herbs for Achieving Goals

Acacia
Allspice
Aloe
Angelica
Anise
Blueberry
Caraway
Cherry
Clover
Coriander
Cucumber
Dill
Fennel

Ginseng
Henna
Juniper 🖐
Mace
Mistletoe 🖐
Mustard
Nutmeg
Plantain 🖐
Pomegranate
Poppy
Star Anise
Strawberry
Sunflower

Herbs for Prosperity

Acacia
Almond
Anise

Basil
Bayberry
Cassia

Chamomile
Cinnamon
Cinquefoil
Clover
Comfrey
Garlic
Ginseng
Honeysuckle
Irish Moss
Lavender

Marigold
Myrtle
Nutmeg
Orange
Peppermint 🖐
Solomon's Seal
Spearmint
Sunflower
Thyme
Wintergreen 🖐

Herbs for Luck

Anise
Agrimony
Bay
Cassia
Chamomile
Cinnamon
Clover
Dandelion 🖐
Frankincense
Honeysuckle
Lavender
Mace
Marigold
Mistletoe 🖐

Myrrh
Nutmeg
Orange
Peppermint 🖐
Rose
Rosemary
St. John's Wort 🖐
Sandalwood
Spearmint 🖐
Solomon's Seal
Sunflower
Violet
Wintergreen 🖐
Yarrow 🖐

Herbs for Cooperation and Harmony

Acacia

Althea

Basil

Calamus

Catnip

Chamomile

Cinnamon

Hibiscus

Lavender

Lemon Verbena

Lilac

Marjoram

Motherwort

Oregano

Poppy

Primrose

Rose

Sage

Violet

Herbs for Protection

Acacia

Agrimony

Angelica

Anise

Asafoetida

Balm of Gilead

Basil

Bay

Bergamot

Bindweed

Broom

Caraway

Cassia

Cinnamon

Cinquefoil

Clover

Cloves

Comfrey

Cranesbill

Dill

Dogwood

Elder

Eucalyptus

Fennel

Frankincense

Garlic

Hemlock

Hyssop

Irish Moss

Juniper ✍

Lavender

Lemon Verbena

Lovage

Mandrake 🖐

Marigold

Marjoram

Mistletoe 🖐

Mugwort 🖐

Mustard

Myrrh

Nutmeg

Oak

Pennyroyal 🖐

Peppermint 🖐

Pine

Primrose

Rose Geranium

Rosemary

Sage

St. John's Wort 🖐

Sandalwood

Sarsaparilla

Slippery Elm

Spearmint 🖐

Spruce 🖐

Storax

Sunflower

Tarragon

Thyme 🖐

Vervain

Wisteria

Woodruff

Wormwood 🖐

Yew

Appendix C

Magical Alphabets

Theban

A	B	C	D	E	F	G	H	I	J	K
૧	૨	൩	൩	૨	൱	℧	૪	Ⴎ		ℿ

L	M	N	O	P	Q	R	S	T	U	V
૪	૨	൬	૪	൬	૨	൬	૪	൬		૧

W	X	Y	Z	&
	൬	൬	൬	൬

Etruscan

A	B	C	D	E	F	G	H	I	J	K
Я	ꓛ	ꙅ	Я	Ɛ	8	D	꒕	꒦		꒷

L	M	N	O	P	Q	R	S	T	U	V
ꓶ	ꟽ	И	◇	H		△	꒑	↗		ꝟ

W	X	Y	Z	CH	IL
	ꓫ		Z	ꖌ	ꭥ

Templar

A	B	C	D	E	F	G	H	I	J	K
∨	<	∧	>	⊿	◿	△	▽	◇		◇

L	M	N	O	P	Q	R	S	T	U	V
◊	◇	✕	⌄	<	∧	>	▽	◁		△

W	X	Y	Z
◊	◈	◇	◇

Notes

Introduction

1. *The New Encyclopaedia Britannica Macropaedia Knowledge in Depth,* 15th ed., s. v. "writing, forms of."
2. Wu of Hsia was the first of the five mythical emperors of the Chinese. Each of these emperors is credited with inventing something. As well as writing, Wu is credited with the invention of feng shui, the I Ching, astrology, and numerology. See Webster, *Feng Shui for Beginners,* 189.
3. Webster, *Omens, Oghams and Oracles,* 60.
4. Gordon, *Take My Word for It,* 89.
5. Jacq, *Magic and Mystery,* 71–72.
6. Webster, *Omens, Oghams and Oracles,* 60–61.

7. The Egyptians also used hieratic writing, which was used by the priests, and demotic writing which was used by educated people.

8. Anonymous, *The Encyclopedia of Occult Sciences*, 306.

9. According to *The New Encyclopaedia Britannica Macropaedia Knowledge in Depth*, 15th ed., s. v. "prayer," there is some evidence to indicate that prayer wheels were at one time used by the ancient Japanese, Celts, Greeks, and Egyptians.

10. Morris, "Spiritual Schism," sec. E, p. 2. There are two claimants for the 17th Karmapa Lama (Urgyen Thinley and Thaye Dorje), and both have many supporters. Consequently, supporters of Thaye Dorje claim that the letter found inside the amulet is a forgery. See Scott-Clark and Levy, "Feud of the Gods of Shangri-La," 22–29.

11. Terzani, *A Fortune-Teller Told Me*, 65–66.

Chapter 1

1. Palmer, *Travels through Sacred China*, 11.

2. Cott and El Zeini, *The Search for Omm Sety*, 81. The name *Omm Sety* (Arabic for "Mother of Sety") was the name taken by Dorothy Eady, an Englishwoman who spent most of her life in Egypt.

3. Jacq, *Magic and Mystery*, 62.

4. Regula, *The Mysteries of Isis*, 80.

5. Singer and Singer, *Divine Magic*, 62.
6. Crow, *Alchemy*, 73.
7. Jaffé, "Symbolism in the Visual Arts," 246.

Chapter 4

1. Webster, *Spirit Guides and Angel Guardians*, 10.
2. Ps. 91:11 King James Version.
3. Matt. 18:10 King James Version.
4. Jung, *Memories, Dreams, Reflections*, 302.

Chapter 6

1. Spence, *An Encyclopaedia of Occultism*, 258.
2. Hodson, *Hidden Wisdom*, 1:23.
3. Quoted in Blavatsky, *The Secret Doctrine*, 5:169.
4. Williamson, *Times and Teachings*, 23.
5. Crowley, *Magick Liber ABA*, 126.
6. Greer, *Women*, 64.

Chapter 7

1. Webster, *Omens, Oghams and Oracles*, 39–41.
2. Webster, *Numerology Magic*, 2.
3. Gonda, "The Indian Mantra," 249.
4. See also Exodus 13:21 and 19:18, Deuteronomy 4:12, 2 Samuel 22:13, Isaiah 6:4, Ezekiel 1:4, Daniel 7:10, Malachi 3:2, Matthew 3:11, and Revelation 1:14 and 4:5.
5. Cave, *Chinese Paper Offerings*, 62.

6. Worship of the Hearth God dates back to at least 133 B.C.E. His picture is pasted up near the stove. His main task is to determine the length of life of everyone living in the house. He is responsible for wealth or poverty, and he records all the good and bad things that family members have done during the year. On the twenty-third day of the twelfth month, sacrificial food is placed in front of him, and each member of the family prostrates him or herself in front of him. Firecrackers are lit to frighten away evil spirits. Once this ceremony is over, the picture is torn down and burnt, along with paper money and requests from the family. A new picture of the Hearth God is pasted up after the New Year, and an offering of vegetables is placed before him to ensure his benevolence over the next twelve months.

7. Traditionally, the Lantern Festival was a time when wealthy people decorated their homes with red paper lanterns and single girls were allowed out to meet young men.

8. Webster, *Feng Shui for Beginners*, 8–9.

9. Williams, *Outlines*, 208.

10. There are many magical alphabets that can be used, most dating from the Renaissance. Theban, possibly the most commonly used magical alphabet today, dates from this period. The fascinating history of magical alphabets can be found in *The*

Secret Lore of Runes and Other Ancient Alphabets by Nigel Pennick.

11. Webster, *Numerology Magic*, 59–64.

12. Crowther, *Lid off the Cauldron*, 55.

Chapter 8

1. Anonymous, *The Encyclopedia of Occult Sciences*, 317. Bezoar is a substance produced in the stomachs and intestines of ruminants. It is believed to be an antidote against poison.

2. Harris, *The Good Luck Book*, vi.

3. Day, *Occult Illustrated Dictionary*, 129.

4. Deut. 6:9 King James Version.

5. Isa. 3:21 King James Version.

6. Fernie, *Occult*, 105–106.

7. Barrett, *The Magus*, 95.

8. A number of lists have been compiled to indicate the twelve stones in the high priest's breastplate (Exodus 28:17–30). They are believed to have been: carnelian, chrysolite, emerald, ruby, lapis lazuli, onyx, sapphire, agate, amethyst, topaz, beryl, and jasper.

   Likewise, the Foundations of the Heavenly City (Revelation 21:10–30) contained: jasper, sapphire, chalcedony, emerald, sardonyx, sardius, chrysolite, beryl, topaz, chrysoprasus, jacinth, and amethyst.

9. Kunz, *Curious Lore*, 307.

10. Webster, *Numerology Magic*, 152.

11. Day, *Occult Illustrated Dictionary*, 3.
12. Nine has always been considered a powerful number. It is the highest single digit number. It is the sum of three, which is also considered a particularly magical number. If you add up the answer of any number multiplied by nine and bring it down to a single digit, the answer will always be nine (for instance: 9 x 12 = 108, and 1 + 0 + 8 = 9). This is why so many powerful amulets contain nine stones. For further information see *Numerology Magic* by Richard Webster.
13. Harris, *The Good Luck Book*, 141–42.
14. Gonzaléz-Wippler, *Complete Book*, 153.
15. Allemann, *History of the Chinese Peoples*, 49.
16. Eberhard, *A Dictionary of Chinese Symbols*, 17.
17. Jia-fong, "Fu," 12.

Chapter 9

1. Fernie, *Occult*, 1.
2. Crow, *Precious Stones*, 15.
3. Exodus 28:17–28.

Chapter 10

1. Webster, *Numerology Magic*, 1.
2. Ibid., 1–2. This book covers both pictorial and numerological yantras.
3. Jaffé, *Symbolism in the Visual Arts*, 249.
4. Ibid., 241.

Chapter 11

1. Hill, *Think and Grow Rich*, 169.
2. Fortune, *Applied Magic*, 21.
3. Butler, *The Magician*, 16.

Chapter 12

1. Mathers, *Key of Solomon*, 48.
2. The SATOR square is the best-known example of a lettered magic square. According to *The New Encyclopaedia Britannica Micropaedia* it was still being used in the nineteenth century in Europe and the United States for protection against fire, sickness, and other calamities. The word *tenet* is in the center horizontally and vertically, creating a hidden cross. 15th ed., s. v. "magic square."

Bibliography

Works Cited

Allemann, D. W. *History of the Chinese Peoples*. Hong Kong: Brockfield and Aberhart, 1903.

Anonymous (M. C. Poinsot). *The Encyclopedia of Occult Sciences*. 1939. Reprint, New York: Tudor Publishing Company, n.d.

Barrett, Francis. *The Magus*. 1801. Reprint, Wellingborough, Northamptonshire: The Aquarian Press, 1989.

Blavatsky, H. P. *The Secret Doctrine*. Vol. 5. N.p.: Adyar Publishing House, n.d.

Butler, W. E. *The Magician: His Training and Work*. London: The Aquarian Press, 1959.

Cave, Roderick. *Chinese Paper Offerings*. Hong Kong: Oxford University Press, 1998.

Cott, Jonathan, and Henry El Zeini. *The Search for Omm Sety.* New York: Warner Books, Inc., 1989.

Crow, J. H. *Alchemy.* London: Barker and Company, 1884.

Crow, W. B. *Precious Stones.* Wellingborough, Northamptonshire: The Aquarian Press, 1968.

Crowley, Aleister. *Magick Liber ABA.* Book 4. 1913. Reprint, York Beach, Maine: Samuel Weiser, Inc., 1994.

Crowther, Patricia. *Lid off the Cauldron.* York Beach, Maine: Samuel Weiser, Inc., 1983.

Day, Harvey. *Occult Illustrated Dictionary.* London: Kaye and Ward Limited, 1975.

Eberhard, Wolfram. *A Dictionary of Chinese Symbols.* London: Routledge and Kegan Paul Limited, 1986.

Fernie, William T., M.D. *The Occult and Curative Powers of Precious Stones.* 1907. Reprint, San Francisco: Harper and Row Publishers, 1981.

Fortune, Dion. *Applied Magic and Aspects of Occultism.* Wellingborough, Northamptonshire: The Aquarian Press, 1987.

Gonda, Jan. "The Indian Mantra." In *Selected Studies.* Leiden, the Netherlands: E. J. Brill, 1975.

González-Wippler, Migene. *The Complete Book of Spells, Ceremonies and Magic.* New York: Crown Publishers, Inc., 1978.

Gordon, Ian. *Take My Word for It.* Auckland, New Zealand: Wilson and Horton Publications, 1997.

Greer, Mary K. *Women of the Golden Dawn: Rebels and Priestesses*. Rochester, Vt.: Park Street Press, 1995.

Harris, Bill. *The Good Luck Book*. Owings Mills, Maryland: Ottenheimer Publishers, Inc., 1996.

Hill, Napoleon. *Think and Grow Rich*. 1937. Reprint, New York: Fawcett World Library, 1969.

Hodson, Geoffrey. *The Hidden Wisdom in the Holy Bible, Vol. 1*. Madras: Theosophical Publishing House, 1963.

Jacq, Christian. *Magic and Mystery in Ancient Egypt*. Translated by Janet M. Davis. London: Souvenir Press, 1998.

Jaffé, Aniela. "Symbolism in the Visual Arts." In *Man and His Symbols*, edited by Carl G. Jung. Reprint, London: Arakana Books, 1990.

Jia-fong, Wang. "Fu: Do Chinese Charms Really Work?" In *Trademarks of the Chinese*. Vol. 2. Taipei, Taiwan: Sinorama Magazine, 1994.

Jung, C. G. *Memories, Dreams, Reflections*. London: Collins and Routledge & Kegan Paul, 1963.

Kunz, George Frederick. *The Curious Lore of Precious Stones*. Philadelphia, Penn.: J. B. Lippincott Company, 1913.

Mathers, S. L. MacGregor, trans. and ed. *The Key of Solomon*. York Beach, Maine: Samuel Weiser, Inc., 1976.

Morris, Jenny. "Spiritual Schism." *Weekend Herald* (Auckland, New Zealand), 22 January 2000.

Palmer, Martin. *Travels through Sacred China*. London: Thorsons, 1996.

Pennick, Nigel. *The Secret Lore of Runes and Other Ancient Alphabets*. London: Rider and Company, 1991.

Regula, de Traci. *The Mysteries of Isis*. St. Paul, Minn.: Llewellyn Publications, 1995.

Scott-Clark, Cathy, and Adrian Levy. "Feud of the Gods of Shangri-La." *The Sunday Times Magazine* (London), 30 January 2000.

Singer, André, and Lynette Singer. *Divine Magic: The World of the Supernatural*. London: Boxtree Limited, 1995.

Spence, Lewis. *An Encyclopaedia of Occultism*. Secaucus, N.J.: The Citadel Press, 1960.

Terzani, Tiziano. *A Fortune-Teller Told Me*. Translated by Joan Krakover Hall. London: HarperCollins Publishers, 1997.

Webster, Richard. *Feng Shui for Beginners*. St. Paul, Minn.: Llewellyn Publications, 1997.

———. *Numerology Magic*. St. Paul, Minn.: Llewellyn Publications, 1995.

———. *Omens, Oghams and Oracles*. St. Paul, Minn.: Llewellyn Publications, 1995.

———. *Spirit Guides and Angel Guardians*. St. Paul, Minn.: Llewellyn Publications, 1998.

Williams, C. A. S. *Outlines of Chinese Symbolism and Art Motives*. Revised ed. Shanghai: Kelly and Walsh Limited, 1941.

Williamson, J. *The Times and Teachings of Jesus the Christ.* London: Longman, Green and Company, 1912.

Suggested Reading

Bonewitz, Ra. *Cosmic Crystals.* Wellingborough, Northamptonshire: Turnstone Press Limited, 1983.

Bowman, Catherine. *Crystal Ascension.* St. Paul, Minn.: Llewellyn Publications, 1996.

Buckland, Ray. *Advanced Candle Magick.* St. Paul, Minn.: Llewellyn Publications, 1996.

DeJong, Lana. *Candlefire.* Cottonwood, Ariz.: Esoteric Publications, 1973.

Griffin, Judy. *Mother Nature's Herbal.* St. Paul, Minn.: Llewellyn Publications, 1997.

K, Amber. *True Magick: A Beginner's Guide.* St. Paul, Minn.: Llewellyn Publications, 1990.

Markham, Ursula. *The Crystal Workbook.* Wellingborough, Northamptonshire: The Aquarian Press, 1988.

McCoy, Edain. *Making Magick: What It Is and How It Works.* St. Paul, Minn.: Llewellyn Publications, 1997.

Poole, W. T. *Private Dowding.* London: Rider and Company, Ltd., 1918.

Regis, Riza. *How to Manifest Prosperity with Crystals.* Manila, Philippines: InterSelf Foundation, 1996.

Rubin, Samuel. *The Secret Science of Covert Inks.* Port Townsend, Wash.: Loompanics Unlimited, 1987.

Shastri, Rakesh. *Indian Gemmology.* New Delhi, India: Sahni Publications, 1997.

Smith, Steven R. *Wylundt's Book of Incense.* York Beach, Maine: Samuel Weiser, Inc., 1989.

Voillot, Patrick. *Diamonds and Precious Stones.* New York: Harry N. Abrams, Inc., 1997.

Index

☾ REACH FOR THE MOON

Llewellyn publishes hundreds of books on your favorite subjects! To get these exciting books, including the ones on the following pages, check your local bookstore or order them directly from Llewellyn.

ORDER BY PHONE
- Call toll-free within the U.S. and Canada, 1-800-THE MOON
- In Minnesota, call (651) 291-1970
- We accept VISA, MasterCard, and American Express

ORDER BY MAIL
- Send the full price of your order (MN residents add 7% sales tax) in U.S. funds, plus postage & handling to:

  Llewellyn Worldwide
  P.O. Box 64383, Dept. 0-7387-0001-0
  St. Paul, MN 55164–0383, U.S.A.

POSTAGE & HANDLING
- **Standard** (U.S., Mexico, & Canada)

If your order is:

  $20.00 or under, add $5.00
  $20.01–$100.00, add $6.00
  Over $100.00, shipping is free

(Continental U.S. orders ship UPS. AK, HI, PR, & P.O. Boxes ship USPS 1st class. Mex. & Can. ship PMB.)

- **Second Day Air** (Continental U.S. only): $10.00 for one book + $1.00 per each additional book
- **Express** (AK, HI, & PR only) [Not available for P.O. Box delivery. For street address delivery only.]: $15.00 for one book + $1.00 per each additional book
- **International Surface Mail:** Add $1.00 per item
- **International Airmail:** Books—Add the retail price of each item; Non-book items—Add $5.00 per item

Please allow 4–6 weeks for delivery on all orders.
Postage and handling rates subject to change.

DISCOUNTS

We offer a 20% discount to group leaders or agents. You must order a minimum of 5 copies of the same book to get our special quantity price.

FREE CATALOG

Get a free copy of our color catalog, *New Worlds of Mind and Spirit*. Subscribe for just $10.00 in the United States and Canada ($30.00 overseas, airmail). Many bookstores carry *New Worlds*—ask for it!

Visit our website at www.llewellyn.com for more information.

How to Get Everything You Ever Wanted

ADRIAN CALABRESE, PH.D.

When Adrian Calabrese's faithful car bit the dust, she was broke and had already maxed out seven credit cards. She went looking for her dream car anyway, and by the end of the day she was the proud owner of a shiny Jeep Cherokee. It was all because she had found the secret formula for getting what she wanted. Not long after that, money began flowing in her direction, and she paid off all her debts and her life turned around. Now she shares her powerful method of applying ancient concepts of inner wisdom to everyday life. Starting today, anyone can begin immediately to get everything out of life he or she desires.

1-56718-119-8
288 pp., 7½ x 9⅛   **$14.95**

Omens, Oghams & Oracles

Divination in the
Druidic Tradition

RICHARD WEBSTER

Although hundreds of books have been written about the Celts and the druids, no book has focused exclusively on Celtic divination—until now. *Omens, Oghams & Oracles* covers the most important and practical methods of divination in the Celtic and druidic traditions, two of which have never before been published: an original system of divining using the druidic Ogham characters, and "Arthurian divination," which employs a geomantic oracle called druid sticks.

Even if you have no knowledge or experience with any form of divination, this book will show you how to create and use the twenty-five Ogham *fews* and the druid sticks immediately to gain accurate and helpful insights into your life. This book covers divination through sky stones, touchstones, bodhran drums, and other means, with details on how to make these objects and sample readings to supplement the text. Beautiful illustrations of cards made from the Oghams, geomantic figures, and more enhance this clear and informative book.

1-56718-800-1
224 pp., 7 x 10 $12.95

Soul Mates

Understanding Relationships Across Time

RICHARD WEBSTER

The eternal question: how do you find your soul mate—that special, magical person with whom you have spent many previous incarnations? Popular metaphysical author Richard Webster explores every aspect of the soul mate phenomenon in his newest release.

The incredible soul mate connection allows you and your partner to progress even further with your souls' growth and development with each incarnation. *Soul Mates* begins by explaining reincarnation, karma, and the soul, and prepares you to attract your soul mate to you. After reading examples of soul mates from the author's own practice, and famous soul mates from history, you will learn how to recall your past lives. In addition, you will gain valuable tips on how to strengthen your relationship so it grows stronger and better as time goes by.

1-56718-789-7
216 pp., 6 x 9 $12.95

Spirit Guides
& Angel Guardians
Contact Your Invisible Helpers

RICHARD WEBSTER

Invisible helpers are available to all of us; in fact, we all regularly receive messages from our guardian angels and spirit guides but usually fail to recognize them. This book will help you to realize when this occurs. You will see your spiritual and personal growth take a huge leap forward as soon as you welcome your angels and guides into your life. This book contains numerous case studies that show how angels have touched the lives of others, just like yourself. Experience more fun, happiness, and fulfillment than ever before. Other people will also notice the difference as you become calmer, more relaxed, and more loving than ever before.

1-56718-795-1
368 pp., 5³⁄₁₆ x 8   **$9.95**

Spanish edition:
Angeles Guardianes y Guías Espirituales

1-56718-786-2   **$12.95**

Success Secrets
Letters to Matthew

RICHARD WEBSTER

Rekindle your passion for your life's work. Matthew is lacking vision and passion in his life. His marriage is on the rocks and his boss is worried about Matthew's falling sales figures. Just as he is feeling the lowest he has felt in years, he goes to his mailbox and finds an envelope addressed to him, with no return address and no stamp. He instantly recognizes the handwriting as that of his old history teacher from high school. Wouldn't Mr. Nevin be dead by now? Why would Matthew get a letter from him after thirty years?

The letter and the others that follow are the backbone of this little book. Each one gives Matthew encouragement and new ways to deal with his life.

This little book is a quick read about following your dreams, setting goals, overcoming obstacles, pushing yourself even further, and making work fun.

1-56718-788-9
168 pp., 5³⁄₁₆ x 8 $7.95

To order, call 1-800-THE MOON
Prices subject to change without notice

Palm Reading for Beginners

*Find the Future in
the Palm of Your Hand*

RICHARD WEBSTER

Announce in any gathering that you read palms and you will be flocked by people thrilled to show you their hands. When you are have finished *Palm Reading for Beginners*, you will be able to look at anyone's palm (including your own) and confidently and effectively tell them about their personality, love life, hidden talents, career options, prosperity, and health.

Palmistry is possibly the oldest of the occult sciences, with basics principles that have not changed in 2,600 years. This step-by-step guide clearly explains the basics, as well as advanced research conducted in the past few years on such subjects as dermatoglyphics.

1-56718-791-9
264 pp., 5³⁄₁₆ x 8, illus.   **$9.95**

Feng Shui for Beginners

Successful Living by Design

RICHARD WEBSTER

Not advancing fast enough in your career? Maybe your desk is located in a "negative position." Wish you had a more peaceful family life? Hang a mirror in your dining room and watch what happens. Is money flowing out of your life rather than into it? You may want to look to the construction of your staircase!

For thousands of years, the ancient art of feng shui has helped people harness universal forces and lead lives rich in good health, wealth, and happiness. The basic techniques in *Feng Shui for Beginners* are very simple, and you can put them into place immediately in your home and work environments. Gain peace of mind, a quiet confidence, and turn adversity to your advantage with feng shui remedies.

1-56718-803-6
240 pp., 5¼ x 8, photos, diagrams   **$12.95**

To order, call 1-800-THE MOON
Prices subject to change without notice

Feng Shui for
Success & Happiness

RICHARD WEBSTER

"If you want to be happy," a wise man once said, "be happy!"
However, it is not always easy to remain happy when your
environment is working against you. Your home should be a
place where you can completely be yourself.

The ancient Chinese noticed that different environments had
a direct bearing on contentment and even luck. Later on, these
factors would become known as feng shui, the art of living in
harmony with the earth. Whether you live in a one-room apartment or a sprawling mansion, *Feng Shui for Success & Happiness*
(part of Richard Webster's *Feng Shui* series), will show you how
to activate the energy, or ch'i, in your home to improve your
environment and to achieve happiness and abundance.

1-56718-815-X
168 pp., 5¼ x 8, illus.   **$9.95**

Spanish edition:
Feng Shui para el Éxito y la Felicidad

1-56718-820-6   **$7.95**

To order, call 1-800-THE MOON
Prices subject to change without notice

Feng Shui for Love & Romance

RICHARD WEBSTER

For thousands of years, the Chinese have known that if they arrange their homes and possessions in the right way, they will attract positive energy into their life, including a life rich in love and friendship. Now you can take advantage of this ancient knowledge so you can attract the right partner to you; if you're currently in a relationship, you can strengthen the bond between you and your beloved.

It's amazingly simple and inexpensive. Want your partner to start listening to you? Display some yellow flowers in the *Ken* (communication) area of your home. Do you want to bring more friends of both sexes into your life? Place some green plants or candles in the *Chien* (friendship) area. Is your relationship good in most respects but lacking passion between the sheets? Be forewarned—once you activate *this* area with feng shui, you may have problems getting enough sleep at night!

1-56718-792-7
192 pp., 5¼ x 8 $9.95